10/11 -13

X

DRIVE, THEY SAID

······································

DRIVE, THEY SAID

Poems about Americans
and Their Cars

Edited by Kurt Brown

Preface by
Edward Hirsch

MILKWEED
EDITIONS

Thanks to Jim Finnegan for his help at the outset; Alexis Sears for her deluxe
typing; Emilie Buchwald of Milkweed Editions for her patience, understanding, and
expertise; and Edward Hirsch for his inspirational friendship.
Special thanks to Kelleen Zubick, without whom this project
would have run out of gas.

Publication of this book is made possible in part by grants provided by the Jerome Foundation;
the Minnesota State Arts Board through an appropriation by the Minnesota State Legislature;
and the Literature Program of the National Endowment for the Arts. Additional support has
been provided by the Elmer and Eleanor Andersen Foundation; Dayton Hudson Foundation for
Dayton's and Target Stores; First Bank System Foundation; General Mills Foundation;
Honeywell Foundation; John S. and James L. Knight Foundation; The McKnight Foundation;
Andrew W. Mellon Foundation; Challenge Program of the National Endowment for the Arts;
Northwest Area Foundation; I. A. O'Shaughnessy Foundation; Piper Family Fund of the
Minneapolis Foundation; Piper Jaffray Companies, Inc.; John and Beverly Rollwagen Fund; Star
Tribune/Cowles Media Foundation; Surdna Foundation; James R. Thorpe Foundation; Unity
Avenue Foundation; Lila Wallace-Reader's Digest Literary Publishers Marketing Development
Program, funded through a grant to the Council of Literary Magazines and Small Presses;
and generous individuals.

Library of Congress Cataloging-in-Publication Data

Drive, they said : poems about Americans and their cars / edited by Kurt Brown.—1st ed.
    p. cm.
    ISBN 0-915943-90-5
    1. Automobile driving—United States—Poetry. 2. Automobiles—United States—
Poetry. 3. American poetry—20th century.
I. Brown, Kurt.
PS595.A87D75 1994
811'.5080356—dc20   93-33856
                                                                             CIP

This book is dedicated to Maëlle de Schutter-Bosselaar

I must follow you over this long road . . .

I Know a Man

As I sd to my
friend, because I am
always talking,—John, I

sd, which was not his
name, the darkness sur-
rounds us, what

can we do against
it, or else, shall we &
why not, buy a goddamn big car,

drive, he sd, for
christ's sake, look
out where yr going.

—Robert Creeley

Contents

The Great Escape

Men in Cars

Women in Cars

Driving into Yourself

Stopping by the Side of the Road

Head On

Driving as Metaphor

On the Bus

Passing Through

Preface

THE AUTOMOBILE is such a central, constitutive feature of American life that it has become an emblem in our poetry, an odd, moving, sometimes comical and sometimes deadly serious icon of our geographical space and allotted time. Who are we with our famous innocence and touching faith in the transforming powers of technology, our consuming (and consumer) dreams, our belated idea of the Open Road? And how much of our communal character is shared by individual writers? In his now-classic *Studies in American Literature* (1923), D. H. Lawrence perceptively uses automotive terms to describe Walt Whitman's determined New World vision. Lawrence writes:

> He drove an automobile with a very fierce headlight, along the track of a fixed idea, through the darkness of this world. And he saw everything that way. Just as a motorist does in the night . . .
>
> I, seeing Walt go by in his great fierce poetic machine, think to myself: What a funny world that fellow sees!
>
> ONE DIRECTION! toots Walt in the car, whizzing along it . . .
>
> ONE DIRECTION! whoops America, and sets off also in an automobile.

Whitman's optimistic dynamism doesn't seem far behind us, and yet how much more difficult it has become to affirm our one-directional mentality, our whooping commitment to progress, our good-natured setting forth without thinking. The world has changed, not always for the better, and we have done our best to change it, regardless of the consequences. At the conclusion of his diagnostic lyric, "To Elsie," William Carlos Williams reaches out for a figure that will epitomize our rootlessness, a trope that will signal how "the pure products of America / go crazy," how modern life has been veering out of control. "No one / to witness / and adjust," Williams writes, "no one to drive the car."

What is happening in the contemporary world has not gone unobserved by our writers. The American poet, indeed American poetry itself, has been on the move. One feels that *DRIVE, They Said* is an event that has been waiting to take place, a story scattered in fragments around the country and now happily gathered together. That story has been happening at road-stops and gas stations, it has been sleeping under bridges and walking on side streets in small towns and large cities, it has been pushing itself all night across the country and pulling off the highway in the early morning. It is a many-colored story that has been driving all over America, that has been watching people with some urgency. I speak of the inclusive lyric that American poets, mostly unbeknownst to the larger world, have been singing with accuracy and grace. It is a music that witnesses and adjusts.

—Edward Hirsch

INTRODUCTION

This   solitude   covered   with   iron...

WHEN JACK KEROUAC published *On The Road* in 1957, he was wittingly or unwittingly putting his finger on a major theme in American culture: moving on. Or, as John Steinbeck called it in *The Red Pony*, westering.

The impulse to keep moving, to push always farther and farther into the unsettled parts of our country, began almost immediately as the first European planters touched our coasts and grew quickly fascinated by the available land and resources of the interior. This movement originated in Europe itself on a large scale as the colonial frenzy swept Spain, France, Holland, and finally England in the sixteenth and seventeenth centuries. To begin with, "west" meant over the Atlantic on leaky, wooden ships with canvas sails.

Once in America, colonists had to find other means of transportation to satisfy their wanderlust. They set out on horseback and on foot, later on flatboats, steamships, and rafts down the intricate waterways of the continent, and even later in covered wagons, or "prairie schooners," over the rolling grasslands of the Midwest, mimicking their first voyages over what William Bradford had called the "vast" and "mighty" ocean. Eventually, they built transcontinental railroads to ferry themselves back and forth between coasts.

But nothing would fulfill our appetite for wandering like the automobile. When it appeared at the beginning of the twentieth century, the desire for quick and easy mobility over tremendous spaces in the New World would find expression in a network of roads plied by mass-produced "horseless carriages" that quickly resulted in the turnpikes, multi-lane highways, cloverleafs, and traffic jams of the present. Now virtually everyone could move, randomly and at whim, whenever the spirit struck them. This constant, frantic motion has left its mark on the American character as much as anything else in our national experience.

No matter that we no longer have anywhere to go. When the mother in Veronica Patterson's poem "Every Spring on Certain Nights" takes to the road, "wheels on gravel," she is obeying an impulse as old as Columbus. And the woman in Martha McFerren's poem "Leaving in 1927" tells herself: "you have this wild urge / to just take off, / pack your roadster / and head for twilight time . . . 'Clear out, honeychild . . . pack yourself and scram.'" This "wild urge" is what Kerouac, and others, elevated to the level of myth as he and his buddies dashed from New York to San Francisco to Mexico City and back. The going itself—the sheer blur and comfort of movement—would define a pattern of freedom and quest later broadcast, even into middle-class living rooms, as *Route 66.*

In fact, the quest motif showed up relatively early in American writing and claimed an enduring place in our national literature. By the eighteenth century, natives and visitors alike were turning out detailed travelogues of the New World. Sarah Kemble Knight, Richard Lewis, William Bartram, Audubon, and many others kept journals later collected in various anthologies of colonial writing. Later, Whitman sang of "The Open Road," and later yet, Steinbeck piled his Okies into a rickety Ford shoving off for the West Coast and better opportunities. Thomas Wolfe rhapsodized the huge empty spaces of America, which led directly to Kerouac's vision and work. The whole feeling, translated into theater and song, was passed on to the generation of the '60s as Paul Simon set out on a bus to "look for America" and Dennis Hopper accompanied Peter Fonda on an easy ride through the South towards an uncertain but more desirable future. Maybe *Huckleberry Finn,* that most American of novels, was really about the same thing—the log raft nothing but a crude car on a shifting, watery highway.

Driving, then—relentless, continual, necessary, rolling motion— became such a universal experience in our century it was inevitable that it would find permanent expression in American poetry. The poems in this book, more or less, attempt to define that central, common fact. So much of our lives, from infancy to old age, is spent in cars. Some of our earliest memories take place in cars on a road somewhere, simply going—though the destination and ensuing consequences have long been forgotten. Later, cars became our initiation into the mysteries of adult life. Driving became a rite of passage to individuality and selfhood. Who can forget that first, heady realization when, behind the wheel at last, we felt alone, free, and in control of our own destiny. So much has happened in cars: birth, death, illumination, sorrow, anxiety, joy, the excitement of imminent possibility, and the crushing weight of irrevocable loss. In a sense, all of us in America in the twentieth century were born on the road in the back seat of an old sedan.

But the quest motif, as we ricocheted with increasing speed from border to border, coast to coast, isn't the only important aspect of the driving experience recorded here. Robert Bly hits upon another indispensible element in his poem "Driving toward the Lac Qui Parle River." In it, Bly notices "Old men . . . sitting before their houses on car seats," as if, even stationary and no longer able to drive, we continue to dream of the power and freedom of travel. More importantly, Bly writes of "The small world of the car," as it "Plunges through the deep fields of night," and describes the driver's experience of his automobile as "This solitude covered with iron." It's that feeling of isolation and peace, of ultimate privacy, over which we have at least temporary control that is so essential to the pleasure driving affords. Where else in the modern world can we find the relief such solitude brings as quickly and as easily?

A friend once described the automobile as a flying chair in which we are able to skim over the landscape, traveling to exotic places without leaving the comparative comfort of our own living rooms. Relaxed, undisturbed, we inevitably begin to dream. The meditative quality of driving—especially long, solitary drives—is as necessary and fundamental to the driving experience as the need to get somewhere, anywhere else that might provide new sensations and opportunities. Sitting alone behind the wheel, we have time to contemplate landscapes, and the objects in them, as they pass by in full view on the other side of our windshield. We are able to see America, all of it, from the vantage of high-powered machines, just as the earliest ads assured us.

That is why so many of the poems in this book naturally become hymns to America—not in the patriotic sense, but in the sense of observed reality and revelation. We are able to see America as it really is in a moment's glance as we travel through it unexpectedly—and largely unobserved ourselves—at all hours of the day and night. So after noticing "a Spanish girl in a white party dress" and some men pitching horseshoes in his poem "Passing through Albuquerque," and after catching a scrap of song from "a banjo, guitar, and fiddle / playing 'The Mississippi Sawyer' inside a shack," John Balaban is able to say: "Moments like that, you can love this country." So in "Little America," Greg Pape watches truckers "climb back into the high cabs, / switch on the radio and ride / that rhythm of guitars and lonely women / into the heavy heart of the country."

But the outer world, the concrete reality of America and its revealed daily life, isn't the only possible object of contemplation as we hurtle nonchalantly across the country. Sometimes the mind turns inward, and we are able to drive, it seems, almost automatically as the miles tick by on the odometer. Images rise like pieces of old flotsam from the wreckage of abandoned lives. Alicia Ostriker records this kind of meditation in "Meeting the Dead" when, after twelve years, her deceased father appears to her while "driving / from Santa Monica to Pasadena." And in her poem "While Driving North," Ostriker tells us in an epigraph:

> . . . when I drive alone
> it is the only time
> my mind is entirely free
> without obligations
> it floats from idea to idea . . .

a statement that practically defines the meditative experience of driving.

The first section of this book, then, deals with the essential experience of driving as quest, for both men and women. The basic situation, the fact of rolling forward towards the horizon, the future, the past, a better life, an escape from life, a loss, a deadening status quo, may provide us with a paradigm for life in our shiftless, discombobulating century. But driving affords other experiences as well. Section two focuses attention on the meditative aspects of driving, the quest—not outward into the landscape—but inward towards the uncharted territory of the self. Section three highlights the feelings we have every time we stop, if only momentarily, in our wild rush across the map. A strange moment of disconnection occurs, during which our privacy and meditations are interrupted and we must face the actual life we have been passing by. Now the automobile may be seen in another light, a machine for privileged self-absorption that actually separates us from life rather than bringing it to us, whether locally or at great distances.

The following sections briefly define other fundamental aspects of automobile travel, for driving may be dangerous or ideal and may take other forms closely related to being in the driver's seat. With so much frantic and unmonitored coming and going—unlike, say, air traffic—there are bound to be accidents. Section four takes up the theme of crossed destinies, collisions, and fate by focusing on those moments of sobering terror, or their aftermath, which give rise to anything from fear to philosophical speculation. Our idle dreams are more than interrupted. We are jarred violently awake, shoved brutally into the searing light of reality, and changed forever. Section five takes up driving and the automobile as analogues for psychological or social behavior, our character as men and women described in terms of our most cherished form of transportation, while section six describes the "flying chair" not located behind the wheel of our own car, but giving rise nonetheless to many of the same experiences. Finally, section seven considers driving in a very special sense: as an allegory for the passage of life itself. Speeding through cities, villages, and towns, through many landscapes and lives, all journeys subsume into a single archetypal journey reflected in the experience of the individual.

Whatever the case, it is certain the experience of driving cuts across social, cultural, sexual, and ethnic boundaries, for virtually everyone has owned or may own an automobile and set out, at one time or another, for the wide-open spaces of America. In a sense, the poems included here represent only a random sampling of this pervasive theme in our literature. That is to say, they are selected for quality, of course, but every poem signifies probably thousands of others written on similar themes that together make up a body of literature that explores and records the crucial experience of driving in the twentieth century. It might be safe to say that in essence no collection of poems appears these days without containing at least one reference to cars or driving somewhere in its pages.

Some may argue that by enshrining the automobile in poems we are ignoring the destructive aspects, the ecological ramifications of what now appears to some as Henry Ford's dubious achievement. We make no judgement on driving or the automobile, however. That is not the purpose of this book, though readers may form such opinions—or have preexisting opinions confirmed—after perusing it. We insist only that, good or bad, demonic or holy, the automobile and driving lie at the heart of one of the most universal experiences in our century. No assessment of modern culture would be complete without it. That's why this book is so large and comprehensive. We urge you to read it as more than another collection of poems on an interesting but limited subject. It is a book, we hope, about much more than driving and the automobile.

Strung out through poem after poem you may begin to feel something of the essence, the unique character, the big, sprawling, vagrant soul of America—its empty spaces, isolation, and loneliness, its frenetic pace, its desperate hopes and dreams, the fugitive quality of its daily life, even—in poets like James Tate, Bill Knott, and Donald Revell, the increasingly bizarre nature of experience in a hopped-up, rapidly altering civilization that has made change *per se* a principle of faith. It's even possible that the automobile itself, or at the very least the internal combustion engine, is on the verge of disappearing. If that's true, this anthology and others like it may actually serve an historical purpose—recording, as it does, the substance and quality of such a fundamental activity.

Some may think that driving and the literature describing it are unimportant, even trivial, that there are other themes—love, death, politics, God, war—that deserve our serious attention. They may think driving an unfit subject for poetry. This anthology is not for them. Whether mythic or mundane, the automobile has found a central place in our lives and that is why our century has been described, among other things, as The Automobile Age. The importance of driving, of being able to get into your own vehicle and leave it all behind, is interpreted by Stephen Dunn as nothing less than holy. In his poem "The Sacred," the automobile is presented, in terms that anyone able to recall adolescence will recognize, as a symbol of what we hold most dear in our complex, dehumanizing society—a symbol of identity and independence:

> After the teacher asked if anyone had
>   a sacred place
> and the students fidgeted and shrank
>
> in their chairs, the most serious of them all
>   said it was his car,
> being in it alone, his tape deck playing
>
> things he'd chosen, and others knew the truth
>   had been spoken
> and began speaking about their rooms,
>
> their hiding places, but the car kept coming up,
>   the car in motion,
> music filling it, and sometimes one other person

who understood the bright altar of the dashboard
  and how far away
a car could take you from the need

to speak, or to answer, the key
  in having a key
and putting it in, and going.

—KURT BROWN
SNOWMASS, COLORADO
SEPTEMBER, 1993

THE GREAT ESCAPE

Men in Cars

" . . . weightless in the thick of speed, going nowhere . . . "
Jonathan Holden

Driving Montana

The day is a woman who loves you. Open.
Deer drink close to the road and magpies
spray from your car. Miles from any town
your radio comes in strong, unlikely
Mozart from Belgrade, rock and roll
from Butte. Whatever the next number,
you want to hear it. Never has your Buick
found this forward a gear. Even
the tuna salad in Reedpoint is good.

Towns arrive ahead of imagined schedule.
Absorakee at one. Or arrive so late—
Silesia at nine—you recreate the day.
Where did you stop along the road
and have fun? Was there a runaway horse?
Did you park at that house, the one
alone in a void of grain, white with green
trim and red fence, where you know you lived
once? You remembered the ringing creek,
the soft brown forms of far off bison.
You must have stayed hours, then drove on.
In the motel you know you'd never seen it before.

Tomorrow will open again, the sky wide
as the mouth of a wild girl, friable
clouds you lose yourself to. You are lost
in miles of land without people, without
one fear of being found, in the dash
of rabbits, soar of antelope, swirl
merge and clatter of streams.

Goodbye, Iowa

Once more you've degraded yourself on the road.
The freeway turned you back in on yourself
and you found nothing, not even a good false name.
The waitress mocked you and you paid your bill
sweating in her glare. You tried to tell her
how many lovers you've had. Only a croak came out.
Your hand shook when she put hot coins in it.
Your face was hot and you ran face down to the car.

Miles you hated her. Then you remembered what
the doctor said: really a hatred of self. Where
in flashes of past, the gravestone
you looked for years and never found, was there
a dignified time? Only when alone,
those solitary times with sky gray as a freeway.

And now you are alone. The waitress
will never see you again. You often pretend
you don't remember people you do. You joke back
spasms of shame from a night long ago.
Splintered glass. Bewildering blue swirl
of police. Light in your eyes. Hard questions.
Your car is cruising. You cross with ease
at 80 the state line and the state you are entering
always treated you well.

Expressways

1.

The plaster deer are crying.
Concrete flamingos chuckle
their warnings to iron jockeys
and cement dwarfs;
flowers are arranged
like a parading army.

To decorate is to be seen,
a cube of angora yarn
suspended from a rearview mirror.

Dewayne's head is garroted
on his Ford's window sill,
it chews gum in time
with valve lifters, his duck's
ass gleaming with gear ratios
and torque charts.
A girl cradles to him
As a bubble skirt to a fender;
they'll clasp and unclasp
in the dark.   But her
heart's meaner than her father's:
she doesn't want this bum
forever.

2.

Doing 70
the funeral is an ebony
necklace studded
with headlights.
The dead are driven that fast,

their memorial flowers
clots of speed
in sunlight.

3.

Doing 45 the drunk
fumbles for the radio,
face waxing over the wheel,
and heads for a house
he can't remember.
He'll trot
around the car tomorrow
looking for dents, blood, hair;
half-hoping he'll find something.

Three boys strip
an abandoned car
in the service lane
not interested in thievery
or profit,
but in elapsed time.

4.

Where are we going?
The telegraph poles
tick by, a wooden
metronome that paces
sheer velocity;
the firing order of an engine
our magic number.

A trooper shot
in the face with his own pistol
stumbles backwards into traffic,
his skull coming off like a melon half.

5.

The jackknifed gravel train
has buried cars in a slew of dirt
and the driver jackknifes.

An ambulance trapped
in a traffic jam chokes
its siren into Valkyrie song;
the patient wearing
pieces of auto in his collarbones
moans in harmony.

6.

To see the bodies moving down
the assembly line—
the factory is a slow motion
rehearsal for their real life,
that monster at the Rouge plant
drooling oil and shivering
drills an engine block all at once.
Test track shimmers in afternoon heat:
speed can't be trusted to the owner's hands.

7.

Mother and father drive
through the suburbs,
jaws tightening at every intersection
until they hit the entrance ramp,
pick up speed and
merge into traffic.

Perpetual Motion

In a little while I'll be drifting up an on-ramp,
sipping coffee from a styrofoam container,
checking my gas gauge with one eye
and twisting the dial of the radio
with the fingers of my third hand,
looking for a station I can steer to Saturn on.

It seems I have the traveling disease
again, an outbreak of that virus
celebrated by the cracked lips
of a thousand blues musicians—song
about a rooster and a traintrack,
a sunrise and a jug of cherry cherry wine.

It's the kind of perceptual confusion
that makes your loved ones into strangers,
that makes a highway look like a woman
with air conditioned arms. With a
bottomless cup of coffee for a mouth
and jewelry shaped like pay phone booths
dripping from her ears.

In a little while the radio will
almost have me convinced
that I am doing something romantic,
something to do with "freedom" and "becoming"
instead of fright and flight into
an anonymity so deep

it has no bottom,
only signs to tell you what direction
you are falling in: CHEYENNE, SEATTLE,
WICHITA, DETROIT—Do you hear me,
do you feel me moving through?
With my foot upon the gas,

between the future and the past,
I am here—
here where the desire to vanish
is stronger than the desire to appear.

Sand City

The time Walter rolled the green
    Delta 88 on a switchback
  curve along Cove Road he called

me at three in the morning.
    He'd sideswiped a pole, leaving the Olds
  listing on its side, ditched,

and needed to explain how
    he entered that fourwheel drift. I was
  cranky with Walter, as always,

though glad to get out early
    Sunday morning and drive the Island,
  with nothing left to bless us

but the stark hour. I drove out,
    found him on a street corner, unhurt,
  smoking in a pay phone's light,

so we took turns at the wheel,
    the skin over Walter's knuckles raw
  and cracked from sanding bodywork

weekdays at Kenny's Auto.
    Headed east, we hauled along empty
  streets town after town, only

a few cruisers and gypsy
    cabs left, and the stoplights changing
  insensibly for no one.

On a good stretch down one main
    drag, we gunned it, catching green lights
  way out past the end of town,

then took the black roads edged by
        milkweed and sumac, past the sand pits
    scooped out of the low hills,

the summer homes now shuttered,
        the steeple behind a miniature
    golf course, a vacant drive-in

sprawling beside a salt marsh.
        At that late hour we took in the real
    life of things, how the world looks

when no one's looking at it.
        I'm not sure what comes next: if we rolled
    quietly by his girlfriend's,

and he whispered her a tale,
        or if we circled back the other way
    past the shining Lilco stacks

and wound up at Sand City—
        the jetty where a concrete turret
    stood crumbling on the gentler

side of the inlet, where fathers
        brought their kids to fish for eel, where
    runaways and lovers slept

on the beach. Maybe we crouched
        there on the edge of Long Island,
knowing it could all wash away,

our backs turned on that dim world
        the world of men constructed for us,
    the small surf breaking, drawing

back from shore, each wave dragging
        sand and old mortar into the Sound,
    and Walter, sifting the sand,

said there's always other cars
and marveled at how fast the sky pales,
how accidents brought us that far.

So Long, Tuscaloosa

I give you the eleven lights
of Lurleen B. Wallace Boulevard north
to the Northport Bridge.
I give them to you strung
above the intersections, rocking
in the night wind, red smiles of hookers
making the same promise block
by block. I give you their light
filling the windows of stores gone broke,
skidding across oil slicks in parking lots,
streaking the creamy white Cadillacs
of Druid City Ambulance Service.
I give them to you through the rain
or under the influence: red-eyed, thick-tongued.
I give you expressionist smears
or the acute realism of a December night
so cold those lights would crack
if ever they changed color.
There's a law: the first light turns red
as you arrive. You can count on
twelve empty seconds watching
as they switch in sequence and you idle,
exhaust drifting through the intersection
and up the street. There's the fiery breath
of a dancing dragon twisting beneath
bright paper lights, but where, where
are the crowds of merry Chinese?
All you see are huge shadows
some college boy and his girl cast
on the windowless brick wall
of Bomar's Feed & Seed. I give you
their fierce quarrel, their arms shaking
shadows at the red, white, and black
Purina sign. I give you the silence
in your car, heater fan with its leaf

ticking like a meter. Home, you say.
That last resort. There is your chair
of self-examination, your bed
of doubt and dreams. I give you dreams.
Dream that you catch the eleven lights
of Lurleen B. Wallace Boulevard
just right, all of them green as trees
along the river. Dream you speed
under them, windshield turning yellow
too late to stop you. *Eleven, ten, nine*
you sing out, your eye fixed on
that last light, green, slinging you up
onto the Northport Bridge and out
over the black twisty river.

Hitting the Road

All afternoon the death wind roars at the vents
but we keep to the right-of-way, hurtling
through a rain of locusts and green dragons
past a mole-grey mongrel, partly flayed,
or a flat black carcass where a tire has died.

Side by side we hunker in our blunder-bus.
Its wide unblinking eye's a web of thready
guts, thoraxes, pincers, wings,
egg-yellow, pomegranate, plum.
June bugs ping like bullets off its chromium grin.

Humping in our wunder-wagon, twin lobes
in a padded skull, we ride, neither kissing
nor parting. You sing me wanderlieder while
I work the pedals, Indianapolis to Wheeling.

Traveller's Advisory

Why does it seem it's always a woman,
when you're driving between towns on the road
trying to figure out the radio
stations fading in, out at every turn
until you finally get some painful song,
who drives your mind to taverns and to drink?

Sometimes you're convinced it will work: drink
and you'll see things aren't half-bad. The woman
will grow quiet, drift away with the song.
But you know when you get back to the road
it won't be nearly hard enough to turn
the dials, bring life back to the radio.

You remember times with the radio
broken you sang loud and blamed it on drink.
It didn't matter. Later on you turned
and turned in sleep, couldn't shake the woman
from your brain and that night was a long road
winding into sunrise, another song.

You might get lucky. Not everything's song.
Take comfort in the words the radio
doles out in wavelengths up and down the road.
A slow sweep of the dial and you can drink
it in: Peoria, a madwoman
guns down a clerk, tired of waiting her turn

in line. In some small town the mayor turns
red, grabs his heart. He's reaching for a song
if you could see him. He knows no woman
hurts like this. These aches on the radio
send people everywhere some place to drink,
to sit and say this next one's for the road,

to think about what's farther down that road.
Each day something's left behind, a dream turns
back into straw. No wonder people drink.
No wonder people rock themselves with song.
They don't tell you that on the radio
but you learned it along with the plural of *woman*.

Tonight you take this road without a song
as towns turn to static on the radio.
Miles back a woman pours herself a drink.

So This Is Nebraska

The gravel road rides with a slow gallop
over the fields, the telephone lines
streaming behind, its billow of dust
full of the sparks of redwing blackbirds.

On either side, those dear old ladies,
the loosening barns, their little windows
dulled by cataracts of hay and cobwebs
hide broken tractors under their skirts.

So this is Nebraska. A Sunday
afternoon; July. Driving along
with your hand out squeezing the air,
a meadowlark waiting on every post.

Behind a shelterbelt of cedars,
top-deep in hollyhocks, pollen and bees,
a pickup kicks its fenders off
and settles back to read the clouds.

You feel like that; you feel like letting
your tires go flat, like letting the mice
build a nest in your muffler, like being
no more than a truck in the weeds,

clucking with chickens or sticky with honey
or holding a skinny old man in your lap
while he watches the road, waiting
for someone to wave to. You feel like

waving. You feel like stopping the car
and dancing around on the road. You wave
instead and leave your hand out gliding
larklike over the wheat, over the houses.

On Our Way

—FOR LINDA

Delano, MacFarland, Famosa . . .

I name them and they vanish.
Little towns that have listened
so long to fenders crumpling,
flying glass, to tires unraveling
and men catching fire.

My black shepherd and my woman
sleep beside me on the seat
as boxcars loaded with sugar beets drift by—
their frail root hairs burning
on the broad San Joaquin.

Is this what I wanted, dreamed of
propped against the doorpost
watching the big moon
sink into the quiet leaves of the fig orchard?
Is this it: to be swinging through the lanes of dense heat,
looking up into the glazed eyes of truckers,
or down on a red dog twisted like a rag?

Yes. This is what I wanted;
to be here,
knowing my destination,
knowing it's a long way off.

Lebec, Gorman, Castaic . . .
Gas stations moored to the dead hills—
"Fill it" the man asks,
greasy fingers fumbling through khaki pockets
for a smoke.

Beaumont, Cabazon, Indio . . .

This is what you wanted,
and here we are:
pilgrims under the late sun,
a would-be evangelist
bad-mouthing the silence,
a river of white water and a barrel
disappearing over the falls . . .

Let's close our eyes
and press into this grill of light
until the dead road
opens like a fern.

Black Road over which Green Trees Grow

A tunnel, but the roof is green and some light
breaks through. There's lots
of oxygen; no worms eat
the leaves or your lungs.
On this road coffins in hearses have been
passing through, not parked or stalled.
On this road; wedding party, friendships, family
visits, a childhood summer sunk
in hot asphalt; dead pets, the broken
white line a monotonous Morse code: *help,*

help, help. How long this road,
which side streets glimpsed, which streetlamps
shattered, mailbox tilted?
On this road: forever-for-sale house, a vacant
lot's weeds rasping (were they ever
alive?), half-masted
by wind. No other car, never,
neither ahead nor behind, no
human—mailman, milkman, child
behind a lemonade stand. No road

signs: Rte. Such and Such, So and So-ville 4 mi.,
X-ton Lions Club Welcomes You . . . Just
this tunnel road, this chute,
this track driven down in silence
(no radio reception), alone, so many thousand
times and you do
not stop, you do
not die, you just drive out
the other side,
you just drive on out the other side.

A Night and Morning First Time Drive to Portland

80N rises from Idaho into Oregon until,
shy of Pendleton, the night opens
across an old ocean floor and my lights dive turns
so deep they have cut escape ramps
for trucks that lose it heaving down.
And they only call this Cabbage Hill.

I unwind from Cabbage Hill onto a dry plain,
the air filling with the light before dawn.
I roll down my window, smell the Columbia River
coming down from the North, and meet her
after breakfast, bending west
to the Pacific. My rearview mirror flickers,
bursts white. Light strikes the river
like love enough for an army.

Above the gorge cliffs, something that looks like
kin to the sun—Mt. Hood! Half the cone
is snow in August. Snow over Columbia blue,
barges frisking the whitecaps,
snow over tan grasses waving the river to the road,
snow over cliff green that could put my car to sleep.
What a mountain! I bet it comes out in Portland
as you're walking down a street.

Driving through Oregon (Dec. 1973)

New Year's Eve, and all through
the State of Oregon
we found the gas pumps dry,
the stalls shuttered, the vague
windmills of the shopping malls
stopped on the hour.

The homebound traffic thinned,
turning off by the roadside;
I lost count of abandoned cars.

This is the country we knew
before the cities came,
lighted by sun, moon, and stars,
the glare of a straying comet,
sparks from a hunting fire
flying in the prairie wind.

The long land darkens, houselights
wink green and gold,
more distant than the planets
in fields bound with invisible wire.

We will drive this road to the end,
another Sunday, another year;
past the rainy borders of Canada,
the wind-shorn taiga,
to the shore of the Great White Bear;

and stop there, stalled in a drift
by the last well
drained for a spittle of oil.

The driver sleeps, the passenger listens:
Tick . . . tick . . . from a starlit engine,
snow beginning again,
deep in a continent vacant and dark.

In the Realm of the Ignition

Just for this afternoon
the traffic patterns polish the primordial ways,
so that thinking this thought is almost
like driving home, kind of numb all-over.
I am so crusty and rusty and dusty from driving
the obvious ramp, that safe and silly sort-of drifting
toward a state of perfect adjustment
and not thinking about a thing.
These are simply flawed traffic patterns,
and these cars are driven into the next century
like satisfied impermanent pigs,
and in their stately mission
they are only getting older.

The cloverleaves are folding.
There is an X on this window,
Almost exquisite, the slight madness,
kiss and forgiveness.

I must turn over a new automobile.
This day reminds me
of all the others, and the virgin
lanes looming just out of reach,
the particular gaping maw of this day
dripping in slow or no motion
like a nocount accountant taxing himself beyond reason,
strictly speaking in the tollhouse of grief
like smoke joining the World Sensorium for just a
    moment.
Aug! The One! This new power is very great!
I must buy one of these new automobiles,

upward and away!

Losing WSUI

Driving East, and I begin
to lose the string quartet put out
by University Radio WSUI;

those grave clear notes, making
a Lithuania of these black
Mid-Western fields must now

compete with blurred
upswellings of sound, tumorous
commercial heavings, as saws

sobbing into the trunks
of trees, women swaying
packed with tobacco, creaming

all the sparkling parks
their world offers. The beams
the tall transmitter spits

so strongly out near home
begin to falter now, cowards
of distance, and the rich

stream of kilowatts withers
visibly almost, a flickering
of birds turning for home

through the November air.
And now the voice of your
announcer, Larry Barrett, displaying

no panic, begins to be
sucked under by a quicksand
of muck, money music, noise

fronds at his throat, a whole
ruptured jungle of sound
springing up around the bright

tin huts our minds rent. I
will not be driven to the edge
of Iowa by the urgent

melancholy of cellos after
all. Larry is sinking
fast now, still stately, swallowed

like a pagoda. A last
gargle of vowels, and the inane
other America takes over, goodbye

WSUI, farewell Larry, remember
me to Albinoni.

Cutting Loose on an August Night

Roll the windows all
the way down and keep it
floored until you can hear the doors
between the corn-rows bursting
open with the August hay
and the full force of the packed earth
being unpacked and shredded
up with speed as the center line
pours tracer bullets
at the bug-spattered windshield
and the night's rush outshouts
static on the radio
where New York trails Cincinnati
and Oklahoma City's
cutting in to say high
tomorrow in the mid to upper
90s, low, and a full slate
of night action out there
like dusty fairgrounds
fierce under arc light roars
no runs, no hits, no errors, one
man left, and the entire north
winces, takes the snap-
shot of a cloud
formed like a horse's head,
and you are fixed firmly
in the cool pressure of the night,
the glare of the Philadelphia
and Boston games as sure
as constellations,
you're weightless
in the thick of speed, going
nowhere in all directions
at once, nothing but the pennant
race at stake.

Driving Again

Driving again,
this time Van Dyke Avenue.
Just beyond my window
October wind raises
a leaf from a sewer,
a gray-haired man standing in a crowd
before the Mount Zion Temple
tips his hat, "not bad, and you?"
When I was a child
I saw this church through the window
of a '51 Chevrolet
huddled beside my grandmother
in the backseat, her small
soft hands holding mine,
her perfume and the smell from squirrel
fur around her neck
spinning me to sleep.
Now I pass a woman,
her brown-blond face spotted purple,
who lowers her head
to spit, I see
a boy's words, "Dirty Killer Hood,"
in spray paint
on the wall of U.A.W. Local 89.
Where was it? I stumbled
through the darkness to the door
before I realized
I was waking from a dream
of this street, this smoke
from Eldon Axle foundry, these
motor blocks stacked against
this dull sky. Too many times
I stood on a loading dock
and watched morning air change

from red to iron.
"Gimme coffee, gimme a cigarette,"
a face asked me, "ain't no life,"
another warned.
Here is the cemetery.
Beneath stones engraved in Arabic
my grandfather, my grandmother.
Beneath this earth
grandpa whose sad eyes
could not endure
the pain of legs numbed
forever, grandma
who smiled although cells
crushed her brain.
Years ago, on a day like this,
I fell to my knees
with my father to pull grass
from their stones.
I did not cry.
When I closed my eyes I did not pray.
Now, in a car, on Van Dyke,
I cry for them and for me.

Road Life

Why shouldn't you too have a woman?

Because U.S. 36 has always poured possibilities
through your hometown, you squeal smoking out of A&W Root Beer
using acceleration for plumage, letting the road
tell you your story.

Your prospects widen and hum through Missouri
toward Colorado, farm after farm, like a C-Major chord.
At the 7-dollar Peoriana Motel in St. Joe your shower stall
proves roomy enough for even beginners
lathering each other's shoulders and groins. Daylight
for devouring cows in the corn, thunderhead Himalayas; nighttime
for keeping her womb swimming in the minnows that fishtail
    upstream
hundreds of miles, coming along for the ride
through conversation turning on bodies in common
which it turns out you've married. At Marv's Conoco
in Mankato, money-numbers on the gas pump roll up their eyes
and whirl.

While the radio wanders thickets of cowpoke guitar
homegrown in Nebraska, both kids bicker lightly in back
tireless as static playpenned and strapped down for travel.
The prairie goes gusting away, huffing you westerly
down a pipeline of sunsets gaudy as flags
dyed in watermelon slaughter. Sage-clumps whiz by like chenille
fleeing a bedspread. The Jayhawk Rock Shop & Curio Stand
keeps changing name in name only. Near Idalia's town pump
one wind-devil filches salami clear of your sandwich
and feeds it to tumbleweed. Anne laughs
and you laugh and Tim gargles Pepsi.
Nicky skateboards brief swathes of sidewalk at Rest Stops
till wind stuffs you all back into the Chevy.
The game out of Denver is scanning through bug-splat

for the first cloud become mountain.

Overtaking Rainbo Bread your Plymouth kicks ass, roaring,
squeezing ahead of the fumes—
easier, now Tim's helping drive. Unlike yours
his mind doesn't wander. Nick cruises elf wars and gold,
unreeling *Hobbit* cassettes into his ear, dozens of counties.
Then Tim says he's had it, pulling over to put something down
on his own machine. Staggering in the backlash of trailers
you reason irritably before giving in,
watching your firstborn shrink to nearly a man
on his own in the rearview mirror. The way a bird turns tail,
flaps a while, and dissolves.

Cruising past herds of fur money on ranches
you and Anne settle down at 65 miles an hour
to August evenings from the porch, where you drift closer
to each other, to both boys well-married, to the end of the debts.
Because you're a blur making time
like everyone else you've had to re-invent the wheel,
the birthday, the anniversary—their innumerable one or two ways
to turn things, hold things
that never hold still.

You speak to the Day-Glo Vest Committee of the repair crews,
to the flag ladies, to the whoop-and-holler of schoolkids
sucked into vanishing points on your bumper chrome.

You speak to each Stuckeys & Texaco, their marriage of sweetness
and gas. You speak to a chicken hawk veering down slowly
into a nest of blue trees.
You startle at tires suddenly brought to a boil
over bridge floor—and at a fisherman's canvas chair, bright
    yellow,
left on a sandbar.

You notice Nick noticing how shift-levers handle.

Now that the pavement's half-glaze, now that the family
travels with you by phone, the Volvo feels emptied of traction.

A slipsteam of snow rushes up and over your face.
You lean toward the windshield to sense how your future is doing.

Climbing eastward from Glenwood Springs you follow two eagles
where canyon wall stacks up hundreds of levels
like memoirs housed in a library
including feathered lances and shields,
warpainted bright as a boast
outside Shoshone Hydro Electric. For lunch
why not try the road's shoulder, just short of the Divide
and sentimentalize missing Indians?

With beer and pastrami you enjoy yellow rock
outcropped through snow fallen at the end of winter.
Occasional blazes of sun slur through cloud's lucent moments
while out-of-state plates marvel everywhichway,
enchanted with clifflines. What do the Indians say?
They say flow is their only idea, and that every lost arrow,
every bone in this canyon is happy. Douglas fir brighten,
dim, re-brighten, hovering drifts, illumined
as if roots might emit a light of their own.

Downhill out of the Eisenhower Tunnel
an Impala shoots like sperm
stuffed with young faces and hair, skis on the roof,
the driver a kid who nods, keeping time
to a rhythm he mistakes for his tapedeck
while sucking a blue cocktail stir
and hugging his girl.

How you love them, these touches only the road could imagine!
Because the road still tells a good story
about small figures pretty much like yours
charging the horizon. And tells how, against astonishing odds
often including themselves,
most people get where they're going. Even in the hurtle
and chinook of the vast swashbuckling diesels
you hear it. And, during hushes between,
in these small secrets being traded by birds.

Pickup

Riding high.
            Over the blunt hood,
the headlights flat out. Gunrack
in the back window, radio scanning from
country to rock.
                I don't wanna let you
stop now.
            Joey, black CAT cap over
a thin spot, nestles his up, door to
door with the 4x4 Ram, in from
Nine Mile Corner.
               Do it, Baby, do it,
one more time.
              They talk options:
dual tube bumpers, lift kits,
Holley carbs. Maybe, after getting off
Friday, Daylite Off-Roaders. Or
fog lights.
             Bye, bye, Miss American Pie . . .
Joey punches the scan, and gets back
Wheeling.
             They talk low-end power,
desert radials, Hooker roll-bars,
the whole catalogue. Everything's far
except here: the glow of the panel,
the surge of the tach as they diddle,
idle, and then back off.
                  There are girls
out there, from here to Iowa,
                      waiting.

Women in Cars

"More women have done this than you can imagine . . . "
Martha McFerren

Adrenalin Run

I claim an empty highway, drive the thicket
with a coffee bouncing between my knees
and morning an hour or so ahead.

In all this stretch of trees
from Old Hardin down to Saratoga
nobody's run me off the road,

thrown deer guts at my windshield
with a redneck holler, or exploded
my tires. Only the horses, suggested in

my rearview, come: leap from
edges of palmetto, tupelo, cypress, pine,
horses through water in a numb,

exaggerated gallop. If I looked
I suppose I might be struck and die
within the year, but I don't turn my head.

And Roger, in his cabin, can lie
on his goddamn waterbed and bearskin,
burn his jacaranda incense to shit;

he can check his portfolio of stocks
and fondle his debits and credits
all through the winter. I never believed

I could take my clothes and drive
this easy, loaded like a shotgun,
through the woods and manage to survive.

But even with the horses on the road
in their slow catapult, I might
run the full length of the country,

me and the DJ's, from night to night
as far as California. I might hit the coast
running on coffee and Loretta Lynn
and slam the door and climb along the rocks
and, like the sun, dive in.

Leaving in 1927

The long curve
from Mobile to New Orleans
was hotter than
an overbaked croissant
and you dodged its flakiness
in the brown Gulf.
That wasn't relief,
it was only water.

And at sundown
you're in a hammock
on the old front porch
playing a ukelele
to the same heat
sweating through the screen,
and on the G$_7$ chord
of "Ain't She Sweet?"
you have this wild urge
to just take off,
to pack your roadster
and head for twilight time.

You're not fleeing heat
because it travels with you,
nor fleeing a hurricane
because there isn't one,
though the idea of hurricanes
just could be enough.

Whatever the reason,
an off chord warns you,
"Clear out, honeychild.
Pack your jewelry
and thesaurus
and your grandmother's

Morocco traveling bag,
completely silk-lined
and with silver fittings
from the time
ladies cleared out in style.
Yes, sweet thing,
pack yourself and scram."

And by glory
this time you do it.
You grab a selection
and off you drive
into the Southland,
into mosquitoes and moths,
your windows open
and your mind far ahead.

You're Marie Antoinette
fleeing to Varennes
with a scarf on your hair
and a picnic basket,
knowing your crowded coach
won't reach the border;
or dead Nefertiti
in the night at Luxor,
being snatched by professionals
who'll unravel you
for a batch of scarabs.

Well, it's a change.
Anything for a change.
You could face death:
a feud, a rotten bridge.
Maybe a Klansman in purple
with a spectacular hood
will dash from the pinescrub
waving a torch.

You're very frightened.
You feel so very good.

Every Spring on Certain Nights

every spring on certain nights
when the moon shone persistently
on her ritual lifting of spirits
my mother took to the road
wheels on gravel, the motor dimmed
in the distance my father sat
down to his reading
we watched each other with orphan eyes
asking nothing

once she took me with her
she drove mid-road, watched for nothing,
not the shocking statues of deer, wolfing farm dogs
all night we careened down twisting roads
above the glittering finger of lake

somewhere I jettisoned my fear
of police, being lost,
accident, death, her,
released the door handle, swayed
to each curve, drank the road
signs of counties we surveyed
the close trees, shut lilies, pale Queen Anne's lace
we trailed, riding night, sucking life
from the quiet breathing of cows, unlit farm houses,
rustling ditch weeds
and the rocking road and the wind of us
until the dark, sure figure beside me turned
between the still wagonwheels of the driveway

now each high-mooned spring night
I stand at the window and see my face
with the moon through it and don't drive

along roads muffled in trees
down whispering ditches;
I have my own ways of leaving
and returning, my own orbit

Jurassic

You think time had lost its way for you
You laughed before you thought this

Then the earth rolled under your wheels as
You drove across Route 80 blinded by sun

Putting on shades you startled Ute and Shoshone
(Jim Bridger settled later as the beaver trade dried up)

Muskets, bright feathers, phantom beadwork, bulldozers
Are all implements that turn the wheel

They spoke to you as no other history did
And you "cracked" the window to breathe fresh air

It adds up to a fraction of any life and yet
You are not the Dallas Cowboys, the Denver Broncos

You are not the Washington Redskins or New York Giants
(In the growing incredulity of these names)

You are She's-Driving-A-Car-On-A-Saturday
Observing a dirt-truck kick up a mirage

You are moving down the incline too
Curious and smaller than the rest of the dinosaurs

Perhaps this is the last light you will ever see
Lining the beautiful earth.

Driving to Houston

Somebody named this primitive river Vermilion.
And somebody named the town Boxite,
as if being human was less than what
they worked at here. "I love you,
I adore you, marry me," is scrawled
on a trestle. The names are
painted out. America is big enough
for love, but too big for tenderness.

I am tired and hungry, driving at night
in humidity and fog. Once in a while
a truck parked under an overpass
with the lights on.

At three in the morning, I go through
a place where red and green traffic
lights shine against the swarthy sky
while a black man rides his bicycle
along the empty street. The houses
dark and no place open to eat.
This is the hour of my permission.
The town is called Hope.

As I cross this land, I see no feet
painted blue. No blue handprints
on the doors for safety. What man has
made is a blank thing, a created lack,
a warehouse empty of soul. *Unleaded gas,
Fried chicken.* Three smashed possums so far.

A broken-down car pulling a trailer, the owner
walking around it. Nobody stopping.
Texarcana, Catfish King, "Drive through
service." *Walmart, Discount city.*
A young woman with short brown hair walking

with a sack thrown over her shoulder.
Nothingness with the trees pushed back.

We live alone in our self, close by
the suffering and say, "Did you hear
that bird? Did you see it?"
Yellow flowers under pines, a horse
completely shaded under one tree,
the shadow making it more and less
substantial.

My dearest, you are a green leaf torn
by your own hands because of love.
I could not tell you not to do it,
just as I cannot tell wind or lightning
not to damage a tree. I live inside you
as I cross the Little Cypress Bayou.
I sit on the dry wooden floor of
the damaged shack inside you, lifting
my knees to paint the bottoms of my feet
blue, my surprise for your birthday.
You did not believe I would live
in such a place, empty and hidden away
in the hills: old and empty, never
lived in, or lived in so long ago
it has no smell. You will come to see me
as a snake comes.

It is beguiling to realize I am wrong
in the same way year after year.
To see how exact my role is.
This time everything is clear. You will
come to the small, dry house of yourself
knowing how rare it is for anyone
to find what is absolutely theirs.
You will touch the sides of my face
with the tips of your fingers, and kiss
my upper lip without taking your mouth
away for a long time.

Driving toward Houston at six-thirty
in the evening, crossing the Trinity
River, the sky dull, the water shining
with the sun. You are in the North
at home with two children and a wife.
Here the pines grow very tall
and have no branches except at the top
where the light touches them.
The injustice of your desire recommends
its reality, now that I have moved
inside of you, to let you know
where you are.

Highway

Glow of ice on the dark maples,
shape of a blue fish in the clouds,
hum of tires, stutter of the car radio.
You know the highway is kindly,
the curve of it, your family at the end of it,
the lull of wheels, the sudden view
of a mill town dropped among trees
thin as eyelashes, and the buildings,
small heaving chests with breaths
of smoke. And a sudden tenderness
fills you for the idea of people,
their wills and habits, the machinery
of their kindness, the way meals are
served with salt and with a spoon.
And you think of them as birds
driven by some wind, and such mercy
passes that it makes you weep for it
and soon you can't see the road
for the awful kindness of it, and
the idea of *you*, your name vanishes
leaving you so alone that you must reclaim
it fast as you can in thought,
that dark bird circling over
the road until you are lost, or found
again in its wide wings lacing the blue
moving sky, the car now in motion
past the flash of sun again on an icy branch,
the self safely wrapped back inside its body,
which is your own, driving a car, yours.

Leaving the Mountains

there are darts of final light
flashes like nerves' spiny ends
as the mountain road loops
in perfect rhythm
from right to left
left to right
and back again
again like the pattern
of the windshield wipers
left to right
as you guide with both hands
our slow car careening
out of this day-long dream
of mountains and spiky trees
and rock

the dream is of narrow roads turning
turning as in a dream
soundless upon themselves
and back

in the dusk of mountains
the car's headlights are faint
like our breaths, like our eyesight
ruined with wonders
that have aged us back into them
—the contours of mountains
small enough to navigate
but glaring red and orange and bizarre
as Mars
where the language would not be ours

guiding us out of a dream
you bring us sleepy with dread of falling
down out of the mountains
to Knoxville and a human night

Angel Fire

the sun in a spasm
rocks the car
in this celestial scream
we flow together
mutely

better than marriage!
both of us slick with sweat
eyes aching from the glare
everywhere the world shimmers
with a false sunset
at every horizon

we have not spoken for a hundred miles
as if finally we have become a single flesh
and the flesh sighing with heat
Have we been experimenting with two bodies,
thinking ourselves two bodies?
every pore of our flesh has opened
unresisting
every pore breathes in this fire
spasm of light radiant
as pain
so bright you can't feel it

look, the fire gives another life
to the insects smeared on our windshield!
as if in celebration of our marriage
of heat

mauled by such fire
we are the only inhabitants
of this desert universe
the angels direct their fire to pierce
our eyelids

to penetrate the old selfish tightness
of our single selves
now no vision remains
to turn inward to a single name—
time is only the passage of light
the straying shadows like charred bodies
shapes like large grazing animals
on the mountains
or patches of shivering grass
that appear dangerous

    we have been experimenting with our separateness:
    unsolid bodies that imagined immortality

this fire holds nothing human
the angels in their passion
their belled-out cheeks
their hair dense as flames
hands that strike our faces palm to cheek
to awake us to this marriage of flesh
angels shouting
with the wind outside the car
shouting walls of heat
the slow explosion of heat at every horizon
staggering the rock of mountains
the rock glowing at its peaks
like lava
ancient breathable lava
angels struggling in the shapes of fire
younger than we
more vicious
their fire original and clean as music without words
killing the old selves of us
the old shadows
in one radiance

Exodus

driving you through Death Valley's venom and thorns in your
lipstick red Spitfire convertible racing through nothing
but dead sea and occasional towns of turquoise and shards
to get you to the church on time for your mother's wedding
in Vegas, really lost at half past Dante's View on this
straight and narrow highway of middle age abandonment at 125 mph,
Peter Gabriel's *Passion* full blast with salt wind fragrances
of dust numbing our faces speaking the language of crushed rock,
we both think we should slow down but my foot's stuck
below sea level, my hands to the wheel, our eyes petrified
on this vast fossil that has nothing to do with until now,
our hair trailing us like the exhaust of transcendent thought—
it feels as if we've reached the speed of light's incandescence
thicker than milk sucked from the slow-growing sacred cactus,
as if our watches have stopped on sudden impact with infinity
and we have never forgotten to love until death do us part
while the red paint is sandblasted from the metal,
the metal ripped away, our clothes burned off, our flesh
tumbleweeds behind us spinning in our whirlwind wake and we are
left in our spiritual bodies to ride this blur of pure wind
through the heatwaves between sand and sky

Route 280

In this valley lies
the heart of science fiction country:
some future amphitheater of terror
where the hills make way, soundlessly,
for the thrust of alien metal.

Any arrival could hide over the bland horizon
while we talk in the car.
Your awkward white hand gropes the gearshift
as you ponder, mutter, and heeding, smile back.

The freeway lights greet us far ahead,
set in the calm slope
like gemstones on a bit of proffered skin.

Still, when we reach them
can never be very important. You and I
will always be absent from
our great moments—one of the stars

suddenly plunging down, a peerless
new presence startling us into tears,
that first inkling of another body
easing its way in.

When we roll on the yielding road
we notice nothing. Earth shifts knowingly
with our weight, taking its cue from
the black sky, accepting us
for the strangers we clearly are.

As the Birds

I felt very poor that year,
sleeping by the car, under stars,
my child and the lover,
each in their own furrow,
the dirt humped up like gravesites,
and mornings, wetting the ash
in my mouth, and swallowing it,
the price of consciousness.
We were not bums but bathed daily

in a sluice or by some weedy cottonwood
and we never went hungry or I'd still
hear the child calling out in the night,
desperate as a predator. Still,
we had no home, no work to return to.
The trees thickened to forest or
balded to desert while why we drove
became as absurd as those bloodied nits
spread on the windshield.

But when the child sang, we sang.
And when he cried, we sang.
No radio told us of tornadoes
nor of what else we'd find (sleep,
food, friends) and when the child
napped on the sticky vinyl, we looked
in this same thicket for love,
as if it had been left for us alone,
under the low leaves.

Once we ducked into an empty farmhouse,
its linoleum buckling with dog's pee,
and found the watchdog himself where
the mice had cleaned him. We didn't
pass by to plump the beds. We'd

forgotten about beds anyway,
and the child hadn't known them,
just breast, just the soft hollow
of my arm, so we stayed on the porch
and the rain kept the light until dawn.

There, in My Grandfather's Old Green Buick

He was touching me where no one
had touched me before, there,
in my grandfather's old green Buick
that wouldn't go in reverse,
so all the while I was worrying
how he'd get the car turned around
and headed back to his school,
there as we were under the dark pines
and his whispering, *Some day we'll be able
to have each other completely,* which thrilled me
even more than the touching though I knew
it was too formal for real passion, real passion
made you say things the nuns swore would damn
your soul, and what if they could see me now,
with my hair falling down and my lips
kissed raw and this prep school boy's hand
there, and there, and my heart knocking
the way it should have when the priest rang
the bells at Mass, and the Buick so wide
I worried he'd scrape the paint against the pines
and then he whispered *We have to stop Do you know why
we have to stop* and I nodded, thinking he meant
curfew, so I sat up and felt along the cloth
seat for my hairpins and redid my French twist
and nothing was wrong, he swung the Buick around
and we slipped past the pines with our headlights
still out and when we got there, I slid
behind the wheel and drove down the mountain
knowing something had happened I couldn't reverse
anymore than I could the Buick, knowing I wanted it,
no matter what the nuns said, I wanted it, I could feel
my body wet and alive as if there had been a birth.

56

Nandia

Over McCartys
a crow flies north
near the house
you lived in with Tony.
I think of you,
see old bones of lava beds,
a train going towards
Gallup,
radio fading out
only wind, and
this dry mouth
whisper thin,
like leaves.

We traveled this road
before. Sixty-six
or other names in the time
you breathed. Knew
red rock mesas, Indian tea
stalks dried and empty
and the hardened
black ashes
of the Malpais.

You took me once
to an older part of earth
I'd never seen—
where monsters were born
and killed.
They sacrificed everything
and nothing
for a taste of this
life.

I remember
you held your baby
tight.
He was yours and Tony's—
a point inbetween
hot baked earth
and Oklahoma.

We crawled a fence
found a barren
Laguna corral where years
back sheep birthed and slept
and were kept by an old man
and woman whose children
have grown old in L.A.

To the Rio Puerco
deep blood of silence
where the sun fell
to the western horizon
and your voice and mine
echoed laughter;
carried children.

Now footprints are mere ghosts
washed over in the river
and there are wings
slapping wind
that force sound through me.

I drive this road again
my children older
and this ache
    this trembling ache
haunts me endlessly
like you.

Alive

The hum of the car
is deadening.
It could sing me
to sleep.

I like to be sung to:
deep-throated music
of the south, horse songs,
of the bare feet sound
of my son walking in his sleep.

Or wheels turning,
spinning
spinning.

Sometimes I am afraid
of the sound
of soundlessness.
Like driving away from you
as you watched me wordlessly
from your sunglasses.
Your face opened up then,
a dark fevered bird.
And dived into me.
No sound of water
but the deep, vibrating
echo
     of motion.

I try to touch myself.
There is a field
of talking blood
that I have not been able
to reach,

not even with knives,
not yet.

"I tried every escape"'
she told me. "Beer and wine
never worked. Then I
decided to look around, see
what was there. And I saw myself
naked. And alive. Would you
believe that?
Alive."

Alive. This music rocks
me. I drive the interstate,
watch faces come and go on either
side. I am free to be sung to;
I am free to sing. This woman
can cross any line.

Interstate 80

This SOB never has been an easy passage
Oh, maybe for 20 minutes
after they finally finished the last stretch
around "This Is The Place" in Parley's Canyon
before it started heaving up from frost freeze
or grooving in the heat, but mostly it's a bitch
requiring your full attention
even if you drive the same forty miles
morning and night to work
and know every pimple on the lady's ass
every curve or incline
you could drive it in your sleep or blind
like you do half the time in January anyway
white-out white knuckle terror
braced against the blast of triple trailers
whipping like rattlers in the ruts.
This road will give you religion, mister.
The pioneers took the long way around
but still ended up on this road
near a fort over by the Green.
After bucking the river, the heat
the mountains, the mosquitoes and every other
damn thing, perhaps Brigham Young saw
the look in one of his wives' eyes
like the look a man gets today
when he passes the last rest stop for 125 miles.
Perhaps he saw that look
after crossing the knife-like cut
into the wide flat valley
promising sparkling blue in the west
and declared "This Is The Place"
before she could say anything.
How was he to know that lake was salt not sweet?
Later they got down and prayed
like a lot of folks on I-80

coming through that pass
across a radiator-boiling desert
or around Elk Mountain,
the interstate 20 miles too close
because a highway engineer fell in love
with a pretty drive in the summer
through bowls of wind-etched rock
where nothing lands long enough to grow.
The mountain mesmerized him
and made him forget what he shouldn't.
A motorcyclist crossing the Bonneville Salt Flats
with his sand-blasted wife in the side car
cranks up the Christian radio network
and prays she doesn't notice highway signs
Dust Hazard near Devil's Gate
No Services.

Night Blindness

The seat belt straps securely
over the lump the doctor found
it tightens as I squint forward.
I can't see to drive in the dark.
Headlights of others blur
against my eyes, straining.
Bugs batter the windshield
white against the pitch.
Are those the eyes of deer about to leap
or just rabbits, like me, blinded
by the rushing light
I ease up on the gas.
The engine roars out of silence
like an airplane suspended, about to land.
Was that ever me, that girl
sitting close to her farm boy? She laughed
in the daring night and could see.
He drove dirt roads at midnight,
then, for a moment, turned out the headlights
at 60 miles an hour, guided only by the feel
of surface beneath his fingertips
touching the road, then that spot
where the lump grew.
I can feel it
as I switch gears for the long climb
and dim my lights for what might come
out of the arroyo at my side.

Desert

On I-80 I set the cruise control on 65
the air on max and head into the desert
alone
so different from 1954.
Dad drove the desert
arm resting on wide open window sill
Mom with one leg half out the other window
three kids stuck to each other
shirtless on a mattress in the back seat
sleeping in the car
rinsing diapers in the gas station
stopping to float in the Geat Salt Lake
and ride crusted and itching into the hot night
stopping to ride a prospector's donkey
for a picture
2 bucks sent right to your home
Mom in halter top and short shorts
Marilyn Monroe lipstick in the black and white
tears over a Kewpie's head melting into horror
in the back window, down into the Indian costume
too hot for this country
on the way to Golden California
where I wrote my name
over and over in the ocean sand.

Holding the Family Together

Near midnight, driving a sliver of backcountry road
between two steel cities, I remember the article
I read last week about the awful things that happen
to women out after dark in cars. Outside is only
forest and frozen creek bed, patches of black ice
on the highway, and "safety" has become
the soft melding of gears I'm counting on
to get me home. Thirty years ago, "home"
was only my father and I, eating our meals
in silence by the radio. I was as frightened then
as the small animals, whose eyes shine beside the road
my headlights illuminate, then flood with dark,
in a time so fast they cannot comprehend it.
My father said he was "holding the family together,"
the way Edith Piaf, singing now on the radio,
holds a song together through marching band music,
carousel rhythms, an abrupt modulation to a minor key.
C'était pas moi, I sing along, trying to make the dark
companionable, as I hit a pothole and command my tires
not to blow out here. If I needed help and if
it came, it would be another thing to fear,
like the knife blades my father
flashed through the yellow kitchen,
saying, *These, you see, could kill us both.*
Nothing to be afraid of, I lied to myself,
until he would quiet and tell me, *Listen
to the music.* Piaf's still singing
but I've gone rigid now with defense,
trusting to the wheel bearings and accelerator cable,
holding the family together, in my familiar
numb pantomime of a landscape, in which
no enemy could recognize me as his prey.

A Metaphor Crosses the Road

Sometimes super cool
is nothing more than
pure preparedness.
Like my friend Janet
who was terrified
someday she'd swerve
to miss a dog
and demolish her car
and kill herself
and maybe her children.
For years, whenever
she got behind a wheel
she was thinking,
Hit the dog, hit the dog,
and finally one night
the dog got there
and she slammed
flat across him.

I cried real tears
when Lassie came home,
But I'm worth something, too.
Let's both watch out, dog.

Reasons for Wanting to Have Children

The roads I have to drive at night are unlit,
the only lights are those of cars
in front or behind.

The country is hilly, though,
so the lights ahead and behind disappear
to dark with each hill.
It is an odd feeling, like being followed
or swallowed by some godless thing.

All reasons for wanting children are bad,
and that is why I want them.
I am tired of these blindfolds of hills.

Night Driving

South into Jersey on I-95 rain and
windshield wipers and someone you love asleep
in the seat beside you, light on all sides
like teeth winking and that smell like baking
bread gone wrong and you want
to die it's so beautiful—
you love the enormous trucks floating in spray
and the tall smokestacks rimmed with flame
and this hammering in your head
this magnet drawing what's deepest
in you you can't name
except to know it's there.

Driving at Night

The world is full of these roads.
Absences startle headlights
that set fire in a field of corn.

A white horse
gazing down
white violets and sweetgrass
that is her flesh,
the soft designs of limbo's children
troubled to wander.

Bless the horse
and the clothing left out on a line,
armless sleeves
with nothing to hold but air.

And houses
where women and men
are lying
asleep at night
dreaming all the dark roads
out of the world.

Scenic Route

—For Lucy, who called them "ghost houses."

Someone was always leaving
and never coming back.
The wooden houses wait like old wives
along this road; they are everywhere,
abandoned, leaning, turning gray.

Someone always traded
the lonely beauty
of hemlock and stony lakeshore
for survival, packed up his life
and drove off to the city.
In the yards the apple trees
keep hanging on, but the fruit
grows smaller year by year.

When we come this way again
the trees will have gone wild,
the houses collapsed, not even worth
the human act of breaking in.
Fields will have taken over.

What we will recognize
is the wind, the same fierce wind,
which has no history.

Driving after Supper

The old senselessness returns
when driving in June
the ribbon roads, low corn
on either side, then woods, then meadows
where sheep just stand there,
slowly turn their heads. We are talking again
about how cool it is.
It could be Maine, I say
for the 20th time, though usually
this seems the other
harder world—Indiana—
birds with their *wait wait wait* high
in trees, and such hot dust
when we stop, so studded with gravel.
We pass an old brick school—1880—
disguised as someone's house, the door open
to its ring of chairs
around the small TV, a blue jacket
hung on a hook. Gifts
at every moment, though not
the farmer, farther on,
out circling in his tractor
furious haywire turns, his wife
a thin shadow in the yard; nor the kid
at the next house who spits
on his knife, and lifts it up, quietly now
gouging the porch railing.
We barely see that, joy
being what it is, and the evening
so temporary.

Women in Cars

More women have done this
than you'd imagine.

You're out there driving
back from Grand Saline or wherever
they made something happen
that particular Saturday.
Actually *he's* doing the driving
and you're just sitting there
twiddling with the radio.

It's night on a two-lane blacktop.
There's nobody in the state,
except the stuff that's
been run over, and
already your date is yelling,
"Let's play like we're
in England," and scooting over
to the opposite lane
every ten minutes or so,
and you are so awfully bored.

So you start taking off
your clothes, starting with
your shoes, then your earrings,
then your shirt and bra.
Getting out of your
blue jeans isn't easy.
You have to hoist your rump
and buck forward with your knees
like you're doing the limbo,
but let's admit it,
climbing out of jeans in cars
is a native art.

When I was driving
with a boy named Frank Fallis,
I even whipped off my phoney
ponytail and threw it
in the back seat, and he screamed,
"GAAAAAA," and skidded off
the road. And then he said,
really sarcastic, "You got
anything *else* unnatural?"

You can ride hours like that
with the wind and the bugs
blowing all over you,
and some Wilson Pickett.
If you go through a place
like Scofield or La Tuna
you don't even need to duck.
They're all in bed
with their shades down,
dreaming about rain.

There's simply nothing out there.
Some people say Texans
think more about wheels than sex,
but you have to understand
the distances involved.

.

DRIVING INTO YOURSELF

"The road in is always longer than the road out . . ."

Charles Wright

Mimosa

I can grieve anything
driving these two-lane roads.
The bridge of trees opens so simply.
I pass under and look up
at the brilliant, starved leaves
which must be the color of shame, or passion,
or the truth revealed in stages.
Once I knew something I should have told,
the name of the place my sister eloped to.
In the small wind of her breath
the night she woke me,
she said it like a wish,
like the ritual of the mimosa pods
we used to open each autumn.
We'd count each nut-brown seed a son, a daughter,
close our eyes, and swallow
one for the child before twenty,
no money, the debt
of her young body torn from the inside.
One for the man who'd spend her beauty
in the long delivery.
Then *Greenfield* became synonymous with heaven
in all the hymns my mother sang, hour
by chained hour. *Greenfield,* the rhythm
of my father's boots on linoleum
when he came in late, went out again looking.
Greenfield, that secret destination
I didn't know enough to grieve,
nor the towns they came on and passed through
to get there,
nor the swingsets glimpsed in the rearview,
nor the gathering static on the radio
that was her future,
nor the bottles clicking at the curves,
nor her sudden waking,

nor the frequent stops near morning,
nor her small animal position
of squatting on the passenger side
releasing her urine
as she watched behind her, as she
held on,
though there was no one, engine
running, the dust
wheeling into the kept promise of the sky.

Driving toward the Lac Qui Parle River

I

I am driving; it is dusk; Minnesota.
The stubble field catches the last growth of sun.
The soybeans are breathing on all sides.
Old men are sitting before their houses on car seats
In the small towns. I am happy,
The moon rising above the turkey sheds.

II

The small world of the car
Plunges through the deep fields of the night,
On the road from Willmar to Milan.
This solitude covered with iron
Moves through the fields of night
Penetrated by the noise of crickets.

III

Nearly to Milan, suddenly a small bridge,
And water kneeling in the moonlight.
In small towns the houses are built right on the ground;
The lamplight falls on all fours on the grass.
When I reach the river, the full moon covers it.
A few people are talking, low, in a boat.

Driving toward Boston I Run across One of Robert Bly's Old Poems

1.

Tonight we are driving past Lac Qui Parle toward Boston.
When I think of Boston ladies I am suddenly galvanic with joy!
I see them lying there, pale with Love . . . like flowers . . . like
    palimpsests!
On which we can still make out a few marginal words . . .
Wampum . . . rackrent . . . pui ine o dromos sto horyo, asshole!
Ah—the lemon ladies and the lime-green ladies of Boston!

2.

The parlors of those houses on the road to Boston are full of salt.
These ladies have taken the sea to bed just once too often . . .
And the men—ah, here the Cabots and the Lodges and Lowells
    are dozing
(Dreaming of rum and molasses, dreaming of Sacco and Vanzetti)
In an oily torpor, like the sleep of ancient Cadillacs . . .
Alas! John Adams: desuetude has entered the timing-chains of
    those enormous engines!

3.

Driving toward Boston we pass the Stuffed Ski Surf Shop—
And then the Stuffed Ski Surf Shop—again and again!
Perhaps we are not driving toward Boston after all . . .
Waltham flies by, full of mysterious time zones . . .
I know Boston is on the Post Road someplace in the nineteenth
    century.
The wind is whistling a snatch in the puritan winefield.
I speed forward, confident, thinking of the Boston ladies;
A little of last year's blue blood dreams and screams in the ditch.
Comforted, I press on—and on—perfectly happy.

4.

Whether or not we *are* heading toward Boston
(And even the question of whether I'm *perfectly* happy)
I leave to another time—a time full of lakes—and crickets!
Meanwhile I drive past Waltham again, gaining more time,
Somewhere on the road to or away from Boston . . .
Thinking of the Boston ladies I have a powerful erection!
High as the Dakota mountains! High as the great mountain near
    Fargo!

To a Wall of Flame in a Steel Mill, Syracuse, New York, 1969

Except under the cool shadow of pines,
The snow is already thawing
Along this road . . .
Such sun, and wind.
I think my father longed to disappear
While driving through this place once,
In 1957.
Beside him, my mother slept in a gray dress
While his thoughts moved like the shadow
Of a cloud over houses,
And he was seized, suddenly, by his own shyness,
By his desire to be grass,
And simplified.
Was it brought on
By the road, or the snow, or the sky
With nothing in it?
He kept sweating and wiping his face
Until it passed,
And I never knew.
But in the long journey away from my father,
I took only his silences, his indifference
To misfortune, rain, stones, music, and grief.
Now, I can sleep beside this road
If I have to,
Even while the stars pale and go out,
And it is day.
And if I can keep secrets for years,
The way a stone retains a warmth from the sun,
It is because men like us
Own nothing, really.
I remember, once,
In the steel mill where I worked,
Someone opened the door of the furnace
And I glanced in at the simple,

Quick and blank erasures the flames made of iron,
Of everything on earth.
It was reverence I felt then, and did not know why.
I do not even know why my father
Lived out his one life
Farming two hundred acres of gray Málaga vines
And peach trees twisted
By winter. They lived, I think,
Because his hatred of them was entire,
And wordless.
I still think of him staring into this road
Twenty years ago,
While his hands gripped the wheel harder,
And his wish to be no one made his body tremble,
Like the touch
Of a woman he could not see,
Her fingers drifting up his spine in silence
Until his loneliness was perfect,
And she let him go—
Her laughter turning into these sheets of black
And glassy ice that dislodge themselves,
And ride slowly out,
Onto the thawing river.

Fences

As we drive across Wyoming
the highway's small dead ask to be noticed
with their pitiful feathers, pelts, the red—
and discarded tires thick as your waist
uncoiled like snakes.

There are abutments, small pyramids,
and endless plains of sage tinged
with a hue of heather that seems true color
in the sandy grays.

My son's wrists on the wheel
glisten with sun.
Barely glancing at the bodies left behind
he hums into the hours
as insular as the occasional deer

grazing by wood and wire fences
who sometimes raise wary heads,
the light behind their eyes.

Years ago, my father slowly pulled off a road
telling my mother he needed to rest
while something bore into his skull,
altering him.

My mother sat, hands in her printed lap,
seeing a shadow cross them both.
Witness to her own story
she would explain
He needed to rest, and nurse him ten years.

I have passed my father
at that age
like these cars exchanging distances—

Lulled to my son's music tapes
my eyes begin to close,
dismissing even the farthest range.

The Sunday Driver in Search of Himself

Rolling at eighty, now ninety,
I know why I came here: I was
beginning to feel like a crowd,

you know the ones pinching
each other's fanny, tubercular
wheezing when you turn around.

Whole burping galaxies
of these silly people collecting
inside of me, squeaking,

reeling, until one night, last
night, frozen downtown, I was
trying to recall just where

it was I was going
to meet you, just when, just
who on earth you are. I read

phonebooks, took cabs, waited
in lobbies, ball parks, and
The Tulsa Opera House. Sequinned

ladies, I said, have you seen
the likes of me? Over there,
they said. See, over there. . . .

And, now, here I am, going
lickety-split, hellbound over
mountains, gullies, and water;

and loving, really loving
every mile of it, the knowing
that only you are around.

Walking to Manhattan

Out from a brick ranch house bounded by squash fields,
in lint-colored hat, high heels and ankle-length coat
cut possibly from a roll of tarnished silver foil, a stout woman
strides—farm wife's wide double-chinned face aimed past
the winter vegetable miles that are heart and soul of Hadley,
Massachussetts—and makes a hard left on Route 47 south

where I slow my car to see nothing local
worthy of her well-furred hairdo and metallic sheath:
not the mom and pop store that squats by the dam
or the clapboard church where mice hunt bits of stale God-wafer;
she's not out to impress the five million carrots of Hatfield
and as for Bub's Bar-B-Q and the New Polish-American Tavern

forget it, she's gone, she's walking to Manhattan,
leaving farm-husband dumped in his mangy recliner
mind full of sports announcers, fanbelts and pesticides,
face like a wilted turnip chewed by brown beetles,
leaving one teenager to jack off in a lapful of horror comics
and the other to finish squash inventory in the barn.

The whole unflashy family spread shrinks step by step
as she shrinks in my rearview mirror to a shiny speck
primed to parade through galleries on West 57th: in her mind
maybe she's already transformed Hadley's two-lane blacktop
into Broadway where at each click of her heels men jerk
sunglasses off and taxis honk for a piece of her attention

but there are SoHo champagne openings to wade through,
brilliant painters and dancers and tenors and writers
who lie depressed and obscure as bulbs in sawdust
only for her to discover and lift up and let blossom,
plus the matter of jewels and fur and the right address
including a chauffeur with ice-blue eyes and good hands.

But after driving this fantasy halfway to South Hadley
I ease off the poor woman who for all I know is walking
to the silver anniversary of a friend born like her and raised
content to not stray past the vegetable boundaries of Hadley.
And if her husband snores weekends away in the recliner
it's because he's worked harder than God for thirty years

to transform cabbages into money to buy his kids comics
and computers and cars and college and yes, a silver-foil coat
for his wife who rubs his feet, endures his every snore
and has raised both boys to be better than felons or oafs
and so deserves a coat that isn't as drab as cabbage:
even if she's tacky as K-Mart I find no fault with this woman,

I blame myself: since I was a boy I was bored, bored
by the tobacco fields cramping my hot dirt play-yard,
by dad's bland job, mom's bland cooking, by school
and Sunday school and the whole stupid, humid, tepid south,
so bored I felt alive only in *Life* magazines and TV shows
that showed life in the city, and the city was New York,

and New York was Manhattan and I'd be getting there soon.
So when the teacher red-inked my report card *Daydreams Too
    Much*
I carried it home in a daydream by the cypress-lined creek,
hardly seeing the snowy egrets building nests in live oaks
and was nearly bitten by a water moccasin who lay sunning
in the sand path where I was walking, walking to Manhattan.

Virginia Evening

Just past dusk I passed Christiansburg,
cluster of lights sharpening
as the violet backdrop of the Blue Ridge
darkened. Not stars
but blue-black mountains rose
before me, rose like sleep
after hours of driving, hundreds of miles
blurred behind me. My eyelids
were so heavy but I could see
far ahead a summer thunderstorm flashing,
lightning sparking from cloud
to mountaintop. I drove toward it,
into the pass at Ironto, the dark
now deeper in the long steep grades,
heavy in the shadow of mountains weighted
with evergreens, with spruce, pine,
and cedar. How I wished to sleep
in that sweet air, which filled—
suddenly over a rise—with the small
lights of countless fireflies. Everywhere
they drifted, sweeping from the trees
down to the highway my headlights lit.
Fireflies blinked in the distance
and before my eyes, just before
the windshield struck them and they died.
Cold phosphorescent green, on the glass
their bodies clung like buds bursting
the clean line of a branch in spring.
How long it lasted, how many struck
and bloomed as I drove on, hypnotic
stare fixed on the road ahead, I can't say.
Beyond them, beyond their swarming
bright deaths came the rain, a shower
which fell like some dark blessing.
Imagine when I flicked the windshield wipers on

what an eerie glowing beauty faced me.
In that smeared, streaked light
diminished sweep by sweep you could have seen
my face. It was weary, shocked, awakened,
alive with wonder far after the blades and rain
swept clean the light of those lives
passed, like stars rolling over
the earth, now into other lives.

Meeting the Dead

If we've loved them, it's what we want, and sometimes
Wanting works. With my father it happened driving
From Santa Monica to Pasadena
A night of a full moon, the freeway wide
Open, the palm trees black. I was recalling
How for two years after that shy man's death
I thought only of death, how in April weather
I used to lock the Volkswagen windows so nothing
Pleasant or fragrant would reach me, how one time
I saw him staring in a ladies' room
Mirror, and stood in my tracks, paralyzed,
He looked so bitter, until his face dissolved
Back into my face. . . . My radio was playing
The usual late night jazz. No other cars
Drove with me on the freeway. I hated it
That we would never meet in mutual old
Age to drink a beer—it was all he ever
Drank—and declare our love, the way I'd planned
All through high school, picturing us in
A sunny doorway facing a back garden;
Something out of a book. I hated it
That I was pushing forty and could still
Curl like a snail, a fetus, weeping for him.
While I was feeling that, the next things happened
All at once, like iron slugs
Being pulled into a magnet.
This has been *mourning*, I thought; then a sound came,
Like a door clicking closed, and I understood
Right off that I was finished, that I would
Never feel any more grief for him—
And at the same time, he was present; had been,
I now saw, all along, for these twelve years,
Waiting for me to finish my mourning.
At that I had to laugh, and he swiftly slipped
From outside the Buick, where he had been floating.

I was still doing about sixty.
He was just in me. His round eyesockets
Were inside mine, his shoulderblades aligned
With my own, his right foot and right palm
Lay with mine on the gas pedal and steering wheel—
A treat for him who'd never learned to drive.
The San Gabriel foothills were approaching
Like parents, saying here's a friend for life,
And then they blocked the moon, and I was back
On suburb streets, I was quietly passing
The orderly gardens and homes of the living.

Los Angeles 1977 / Princeton 1985

While Driving North

Note: when I drive alone
it is the only time
my mind is entirely free

without obligations
it floats from idea to idea
while driving north

to read its poems
it reinvents the modern

Something escaped when the pentameter
Was broken by the poets. They broke it
Just as a man might shatter a ewer

His missionary great-grandfather
Brought back from Shanghai, purples and tangerines
Glazed over so-beautiful milky whites,

To watch the hunks disperse, or a man might take
A profane axe to a profound piano
Or set on fire his ancestral house

For private reasons, for the energy
Released when noble objects are destroyed—
Should I maybe have said they "busted" it,

Not "broke" it, though Ezra did say "to break . . .
That was the first heave," because "busted"
Captures the quality of small wild boys:

To kill, break, bust, there has to be hilarity
In such an act, think of the matinees,
A skyscraper exploding, a super car crash

Showing the laws of motion, a villain who loses
His footing on a cliff, this sort of thing
Fine as a trout stream full of fishes sparkling,

Or small boys' eyes theatrically sparkling
When they clutch their chests. A colorful umbrella
Of light dispersed by fireworks plunging above us

And the accompanying boom, than which
No sensation is more satisfying.
It is human nature to adore big sounds

That make the chest reverberate, ka-boom,
The steady overwhelming mother's heart
Being the reassuring first of these,

All others then partaking of its safety.
I mean the odd illusion of its safety,
The same illusion when it comes to speed—

I am doing over sixty-five, the road
Is empty, this is effortless, I could
Do eighty-five, I pass cliffs to my right,

A power plant's two chimneys, tan brick, tall
Handsome, approach me like forgotten uncles,
Drearily sweet old-timers. We meet, we pass,

I think of setting fire to my papers,
The thought lights up, excites me, like traveling
To heaven on a Times Square escalator,

Like love, another flame, a teapot scream
That says: we disassemble in this world
But bubble into an alternative.

Dying people report: you sort of percolate,
And there you are, terrific, your train arriving
At the terminal where many people greet you,

So happy to see you again, you can't believe it,
It's crazy. Up now, up into Pennsylvania's
Lofty humps and bumps, I've reached 380

Where it heads north, the Poconos brown and gray,
The sky meanwhile turning a little pink—
Burning my papers, being free, being happy,

Have I the courage?
When people die they release energy,
Everyone knows, that enters the surroundings.

It's what the person didn't finish using
Or what bound the body,
What buckled its parts together.

This release is called "giving up the ghost,"
And when my father died, for example,
All of us felt a tender spurt of love

He had not finished using, that we might
Use on each other for a brief period,
That could have been poison, but wasn't, it was love,

It comes in through the clothes,
The scalp and skin, no way to notice it
Until after it is inside, working you.

Just the same, when a work of art dies,
Or architecture, if it dies like my dad, suddenly,
Hey, smack, the swing of the wrecker's ball

And its impact, bricks falling, metal springing
Loose and falling, glass dangling and falling,
Oh stay, pleasurable moment—dust, plaster—

So much the greater glee if the wrecked object
Is bigger than a father or a house,
So much the grander energy to capture,

And anyway, they had to kill the meter
Of the old poems, they had to.
Notice how large and innocent they became?

In the true course of nature death makes room
For more experimental life, and the rock
Writing doesn't record tranquillity,

Mostly the land records catastrophe.
Literature the same.

Princeton / Binghamton, 1982

Traffic

Crains, dans le mur aveugle, un
regard qui t'pie
        —Gerard de Nerval

I was driving to pick up my daughter from day care.
It was a summer afternoon and hot, just rush hour
and traffic was terrible, all jam-packed and scarcely

moving ten feet before the light changed again,
crammed in with the hesitant, the nervous,
the cretins of forward locomotion. Of course

I was in a hurry as were the people around me.
But as we stopped again I heard a radio blaring,
and glancing into the car on my left I saw

two men slouched in front and the one closest
was singing to the music, just mouthing the words.
They looked like construction workers or maybe

they cut lawns or dug ditches, something outside—
two men in their mid-twenties. The song blasting
across the intersection was "Stairway to Heaven,"

a big song of the early seventies by Led Zeppelin,
a song that starts with a lot of restraint,
then goes crazy. More importantly it's a song

about transcendence, the spiritual world
that exists beneath the mundane. The young man
was unshaven and fat. Seeing him, the word

that leapt to mind was lummox. Yet what caught
my attention was the man's expression
as he sang—it showed such a wistful yearning,

such tenderness, the child rising to the surface
in the face of the adult. And with the yearning
was the suspicion he knew full well he was a lummox,

that his spirit was trapped in a fat body, stuck
in a rusty Ford in a heat wave in midsummer.
All this was the perception of a second.

I heard the music, saw the young man mouthing
the words, saw his expression of yearning, then
traffic moved forward and the man was replaced

by a woman chewing gum. But this also happened:
here I was jammed together with my enemies,
people no better than chunks of wood, impediments

to my dinner, as I was an impediment to theirs.
And actually the man in the next car looked like
the sort you stay away from in a bar, the fat boy

with a grudge, only too happy to punch your head.
Yet in that wistful reaching out his whole being
took shape. How can I describe the impression

of an instant—to despise my fellow creatures,
then to notice the lummox singing like a stone
become a flower, to feel my heart begin to ache

as if the breath were about to burst from my body,
as if we were all reaching toward shadow selves
that hurry ahead above the road, blowing like the stuff

of a dandelion clock, or wisps of cloud or smoke,
this bit of light the lummox was reaching out for,
which he saw disappearing while he stayed trapped

in traffic in his mortal lummoxy body, as if always
there is the lummox self and the shadow self,
sometimes close, sometimes impossibly distant,

but more, still more, as if this shadow self
contained all he was and all he wanted to be,
graceful and light and unrestricted, while he

in his lummoxy body was simply a mud shape
slapped together by a careless child. All this
was written in his face—that his burden

was the knowledge of his separation. But who
did I see, seeing this man, and what did I catch
but a glimpse, a snippet picked up through a crack

in the wall? Because then the cars moved forward
and I went straight and he turned left and I never
saw him again—cars dividing and rejoining

like clouds dispersing across the sky. Remember
as a child lying in the grass, watching the sky
and the clouds flung about there? What shapes

they promised as the clouds ordered themselves
and came together with suggestions of meaning,
until one could almost see the unifying pattern,

some animal or face one thought one knew, but then
they scattered again, rushed off to all corners.
Yet that hint of connection was so telling

that in looking I felt on the brink of falling
and I would thrust my fingers into the grass
and hang there, arching my back and quick of breath.

A Trucker Drives through His Lost Youth

Years ago he drove a different route.
Hauling in a stripped-out Ford
the white hill whiskey nightclubs paid good money for,
he ran backroads from Ballground to Atalanta
with the cunning of a fox,
hung on each county's dirt curves like a banking hawk.

He remembers best how driving with no headlights
the black Ford felt for the road like a bat
and how his own eyes, groping at first for moonlight,
learned to cut through darkness like an owl's.
Sometimes he drove those black roads on instinct alone.

As the shadow of a bridge falls across his face,
his rear-view says he is not the same man.
Still tonight when there is no traffic, no patrol,
no streetlight to cast shadows or light the center line,
he will search again for the spirit
behind the eyes in his rear-view mirror.
Tonight in open country in heavenly darkness
the interstate to Atlanta will crumble into gravel and sand,
median and shoulder will fall into pine forest,
and his foot will floor the stripped-out Ford
till eighteen wheels roll, roll, roll
him backwards as far as his mind will haul.

Taking a Stepdaughter to College

You have your own car, sleek as a rosepetal,
and I must follow you over this long road to the coast.

You're on your way to college,
an old one founded by the clergy when this country
was a parable of deserts,
a wilderness to cross on their thorny way to heaven.

Already you are leaving me behind,
swooping out past slow pokes and trucks,
as I take my place in a regular line.

Nearly twenty years ago, I came this way
not much older than you are now,
driven by a different need.

I remember almost nothing of these bare canyons
with their scorpions and crows,
these saintly Joshua trees living on ashes and fire.

I could tell you how this land was made—
each canyon falling grain by grain to the river—
how the universities of rock teach time
slowly turning their shadowy pages.

People tell me you're blooming,
and I think of that in this wasted place.
I think of your mother's hands, their tiny fissures
clogged with dirt from her garden,
her brilliant flowers nursed through winter.

Miles away a dust devil rises, spins madly on a single toe,
then lapses back into a dry pile.
Overhead a hawk scans cactus,
studying flaws in the infinite fractures of shale.

We pass a grand cathedral of stone,
its organpipes and pews,
broken tombs for the sleep of martyrs.

Now you almost disappear in the shimmer of distance,
that place where the present buckles
at its edges, then unravels to plunge abruptly into the future.

And now your image vanishes altogether
to reappear in the tiny libraries of the brain, the dark chapters
of our night-thoughts.

I see your face, even now, browsing among those black volumes.

They're right, of course, the wise professors,
gardeners of the mind's beauty—
you're bright as a peonie, flushed pink and dreaming.

Little blossom, never planted by me.

Driving All Night

My complicated past is an anthology,
a long line painted on the plains.
I feel like literary history
about to startle the professors.

But it's not true.

Days ahead, snow heaps up
in the mountains
like undelivered mail.
After driving all night
I guess what it's like
to fly over them.
For the first time you see
how close things are together,
how the foothills push up
just past where you quit
driving. Urgencies
sputter in the exaltation
of chill air.

       Your heart
begins to fall like snow
inside a paperweight.
Oh when in your long damn life,
I ask myself, when will
you seek not a truce,
but peace?

Driving alongside the Housatonic River Alone on a Rainy April Night

I remember asking
where does my shadow go at night?
I thought it went home,
it grew so sleek at dusk.
They said, you just don't
notice it, the way you don't tell yourself
how to walk or hear
a noise that doesn't stop.
But one wrong wobble
in the socket and inside the knee
chalk is falling, school
is over.
As if the ground were a rung
suddenly gone from a ladder,
the self, the shoulders bunched
against the road's each bump, the penis
with its stupid grin,
the whole rank slum of cells
collapses.
I feel the steering wheel
tug a little, testing.
For as long as that takes
the car is a sack of kittens
weighed down by stones.
The headlights chase a dark ripple
across some birch trunks.
I know it's there, water
hurrying over the shadow of water.

Porcupine on the Road to the River

The porcupine walked
last night's double vision of car lights.
Everything disappeared.
One spine after another,
light went out the brittle needles.

Today we drive past,
a man and a woman
talking ourselves backward in time.
Words go out
sharp tongues that have touched one another
rattling an entire life
of salty love
and anger that is its own undoing.

Porcupine, sleepwalker,
that defense quaking the air
breaks down.
In its eyes
we are on the other side of life,
still living.

Behind us the red-winged blackbird
keeps vigil on a cattail.
He opens his wounds,
a sleeve of fire.

I take it in
my own eyes to the river.
Everything reverses.
In the rearview mirror
the blackbird grows smaller,
becomes a speck of singing dust.
The road lumbers and clatters

beneath the porcupine's red and black
diminishing world of salt.

One way or another
the earth is after us.
Let's lie down together
before it stops us in our tracks.
Let's lie down on the bank of the river
and listen to water's pulse.

Toward the Verrazano

Up from South Jersey and the low persistent
pines, pollution curls into the sky
like dark cast-off ribbons
and the part of us that's pure camera,
that loves funnel clouds and blood
on a white dress, is satisfied.
At mile 127, no trace of a tree now,
nothing but concrete and high tension
wires, we hook toward the Outerbridge
past Arthur Kill Road where garbage trucks
work the largest landfill in the world.
The windscreens are littered, gorgeous
with rotogravure sections, torn love
letters, mauve once-used tissues. The gulls
dip down like addicts, rise like angels.
Soon we're in traffic, row houses, a college
we've never heard of stark as an asylum.
In the distance there it is, the crown
of this back way in, immense, silvery,
and in no time we're suspended
out over the Narrows by a logic linked
to faith, so accustomed to the miraculous
we hardly speak, and when we do
it's with those words found on picture postcards
from polite friends with nothing to say.

106

Key to the Highway

I remember riding somewhere in a fast car
with my brother and his friend Jack Brooks
and we were listening to *Layla & Other Love Songs*
by Derek & the Dominos. The night was dark,
dark all along the highway. Jack Brooks was
a pretty funny guy, and I was delighted
by the comradely interplay between him and my brother,
but I tried not to show it for fear of inhibiting them.
I tried to be reserved and maintain a certain
dignity appropriate to my age, older by four years.
They knew the Dominos album well having played the cassette
many times, and they knew how much they liked it.
As we rode on in the dark I felt the music was,
after all, wonderful, and I said so
with as much dignity as possible. "That's right,"
said my brother. "You're getting smarter," said Jack.
We were listening to "Bell Bottom Blues"
at that moment. Later we were listening to
"Key to the Highway," and I remember how
my brother said, "Yeah, yeah." And Jack sang
one of the lines in a way that made me laugh.
I am upset by the fact that that night is so absolutely gone.
No, "upset" is too strong. Or is it.
But that night is so obscure—until now
I may not have thought of that ride once
in eight years—and this obscurity troubles me.
Death is going to defeat us all so easily.
Jack Brooks is in Florida, I believe,
and I may never see him again, which is
more or less all right with me; he and my brother
lost touch some years ago. I wonder
where we were going that night. I don't know;
but it seemed as if we had the key to the highway.

For a Friend

Late November, driving to Wichita.
A black veil of starlings
snags on a thicket and falls.
Shadows of wings skitter over
the highway, like leaves, like ashes.

You have been dead for six months;
though summer and fall
were lighter by one life,
they didn't seem to show it.
The seasons, those steady horses,
are used to the fickle weight
of our shifting load.

I'll guess how it was; on the road
through the wood, you stood up
in the back of the hangman's cart,
reached a low-hanging branch,
and swung up into the green leaves
of our memories.
              Old friend,
the stars were shattered windshield glass
for weeks; we all were sorry.

They never found that part of you
that made you drink, that made you cruel.
You knew we loved you anyway.

Black streak across the centerline,
all highways make me think of you.

Driving into the Hurricane

—IN MEMORY, CELESTE ST. GERMAIN

1

It's two in the morning, and the air in the car is heavy
with hours of driving, thick with wet breath of hurricane.

The highway ahead is black, sucked of people
and houses. A dark thread of road drags me
along the low land to its inevitable end, my beginning.

In the morning people will be leaving their homes in fear
of the greedy mouth of death. They will drive
perhaps as far as I am now to wait,
to breathe in the sour breath of the storm.
Only those who cannot move will stay.
The dead cannot be moved.

2

My father's mother did not wait for the hurricane;
her death, like her life, was not unusual
in the least except that she was deaf and mute,
spoke with her hands.

So the usual practice of strapping down
the hands of the intensive care patient to prevent
them ripping out IVs became unusual,
taking, as it did, her voice.
In the hours before death, they say she made a fist,
thumbs up, the sign for *A*, over and over,
straining against the straps to bring
the thumb up, brush it against her chin.
It was the sign for Albin, her husband,
dead these many years.

She didn't know about the hurricane.

3

Everything's off the air but the all-night
station crackling with new coordinates for the hurricane.

It is moving slowly toward the same place
I am headed, the place where she
awaits her funeral. We will not bury her in the ground,
the water would give her up again; as is the custom
we will seal her in a vault like a treasure
we want to protect from what
we do not understand.

I have nothing to do but think as I drive, as I sink lower
and lower into Louisiana, the land
I love but have escaped, remembering our drowned houses
from hurricanes past, the ripped roofs,
the waiting in strange places for them to pass.
                                        And I can't help
but think, as I drive, of the last two drives home,
the violent young death of my brother, his life
ripped out, the final decline of my father,
ripping the roots and roofs of our family.

4

I try to imagine her dead, what she looks like.
We didn't know her well; we never learned
her language. Deaf, she read our lips and hands,
mute, she spoke slowly for us with hands,
tried with great effort to speak. Slurred and heavy
sounds—she would try to say what she had never
heard. She embarrassed us. We stayed away.

It's raining harder now, the winds are picking up.
I speed up, eager to be home now, heady-heavy,
eye-weary.

I am close, just these ten flat miles of black tongue
over the spillway, and I'll be there; the waves
are already lapping at the guard rails, and white caps,
the white eyes of my family, of family, that
broken word.

5

I wonder how much she really knew, if she smelled
the death and rage in my father's breath, my brother's eyes.
I wonder does the eye of the hurricane know
what surrounds it. Would it have made any difference,
would she have kept on going, like me, knowing,
driving straight into it.

Encounter

Caught in separate dreams two drivers note
Each other's approaching car, their mindless gaze
Pulled by slow hypnosis of the eye.
As each vague shape is lifted from the haze
The rush of metal focuses a face
That holds them as a vision, and they float
In the grip of some half-wished for fatality.
Casually their stares consume the road
As toward some quiet homecoming embrace,
And merge in brief undying liebestod.

Ranch Exit

The roadskin starts to crack
Like a dead crocodile. Weeds chew the shoulder,
Birds scare from my car
And resettle: and this was once
America's pulse.
A mile off and fenced
A fourlane urges you on to the coast.
Only devolved connoisseurs
Of lizards and ranch exits know where to turn off
To savor history crumbling underwheel,
To watch datura spadelike and black
Dig into the runoff, to sense an old self
Slither this drive as if to a house
Now only sleep makes real,
And hand you a taste of the deep white flower
That offers you back the child you've despaired of.

There Is No Way Back

On the radio, an old friend's voice
chokes with anger and grief.
At the Stony Island intersection
I am stuck, gridlocked in place.

Stalled in traffic uselessly
weeping I listen to the news.
The light turns yellow, red
again; a sudden cry of horns.

Salmon in the tide pool, whales
beside the boat: memories flood me.
Then traffic surges forward,
each car spuming its exhaust.

Now the announcer decries
the otters' oil-soaked coats.
I speed home along the freeway
surrounded by the names of animals.

I have fished the Sound, watching
slow fog fall on the blue shore.
—Someone passes me, too fast.
I brake as I approach the exit.

Anchored over the crabpots
I have watched the day moon rise.
A red sun sets now over
the Halsted Street bridge.

I want this to be easier. I want
to forget that oil fueled our boat.
I want to hate the vivid city
as a kind of expiation.

But I've burned trees for wood.
I have boiled crabs alive.
My trapper friends kill for luxury.
Gardeners rub their hands with Vaseline.

There is no way now to be innocent,
no way for it not to be night and
each of us unprepared to pilot
through these rocky narrows.

And there is no way back. There is no
part of the world that is not part
of the world. There is not one of us
who was not on the bridge that night.

I See Chile in My Rearview Mirror

> *By dark the world is once again intact,*
> *Or so the mirrors, wiped clean, try to reason . . .*
>   —James Merrill

This dream of water—what does it harbor?
I see Argentina and Paraguay
under a curfew of glass, their colors
breaking, like oil. The night in Uruguay

is black salt. I'm driving towards Utah,
keeping the entire hemisphere in view—
Columbia vermilion, Brazil blue tar,
some countries wiped clean of color: Peru

is titanium white. And always oceans
that hide in mirrors: when bevelled edges
arrest tides or this world's destinations
forsake ships. There's Sedona, Nogales

far behind. Once I went through a mirror—
from there too the world, so intact, resembled
only itself. When I returned I tore
the skin off the glass. The sea was unsealed

by dark, and I saw ships sink off the coast
of a wounded republic. Now from a blur
of tanks in Santiago, a white horse
gallops, riderless, chased by drunk soldiers

in a jeep; they're firing into the moon.
And as I keep driving in the desert,
someone is running to catch the last bus, men
hanging on to its sides. And he's missed it.

He is running again; crescents of steel
fall from the sky. And here the rocks
are under fog, the cedars a temple,
Sedona carved by the wind into gods—

each shadow their worshipper. The siren
empties Santiago; he watches
—from a hush of windows—blindfolded men
blurred in gleaming vans. The horse vanishes

into a dream. I'm passing skeletal
figures carved in 700 B.C.
Whoever deciphers these canyon walls
remains forsaken, alone with history,

no harbor for his dream. And what else will
this mirror now reason, filled with water?
I see Peru without rain, Brazil
without forests—and here in Utah a dagger

of sunlight: it's splitting—it's the summer
solstice—the quartz center of a spiral.
Did the Anasazi know the darker
answer also—given now in crystal

by the mirrored continent? The solstice,
but of winter? A beam stabs the window,
diamonds him, a funeral in his eyes.
In the lit stadium of Santiago,

this is the shortest day. He's taken there.
Those about to die are looking at him,
his eyes the ledger of the disappeared.
What will the mirror try now? I'm driving,

still north, always followed by that country,
its floors ice, its citizens so lovesick
that the ground—sheer glass—of every city
is torn up. They demand the republic

give back, jewelled, their every reflection.
They dig till dawn but find only corpses.
He has returned to this dream for his bones.
The waters darken. The continent vanishes.

Crossing West Nebraska, Looking for Blue Mountain

Where can one find the real Blue Mountain?
Inside the Blue Mountain at Waggoner's Gap,
is there another, pulsing cool azure light?
Can one drive west and find Blue Mountain?
Will anyone ever live there but me?
Some say that Blue Mountain is very small
and is rocking in the zion of a waterbead.
They claim to find it everywhere, even in clouds
of atmospheric dust snapping with strontium
and settling on the grasslands this evening.
Although Blue Mountain is only as large as a thought,
its sides drop off into dark crags; its steep slopes
are smooth as glass; its aspect is discouraging.
But from its peak, one can see everything clearly:

In humming fields, beetles, aphids, weevils, ants.
Fox pups frisking in bluebells before their burrow.
A naked boy and girl dogpaddling an inner tube
in bayou waters, off a levee near Big Mamou.
Subterranean rocks grinding in the San Andreas Fault.
A Malay fisherman, perched on a spit of rock off Penang,
hurling a circling net into surf at sunset.
A bloated mare giving foal in a clover field in Kent.
A blindfolded teenager, shoeless, slumped against a tree

as the firing squad walks off into Montevideo.
Missiles hidden like moles in Siberian silos.
A black man, in red cotton shirt and khaki pants, his skin
alive with protozoan welts, sipping coffee in a Congo shop.
An eel sliding through a corpse's yellowed ribs
in a Mekong swamp where frogs croak and egrets fish.
Ice sparkling the coats of hundreds of reindeer with
steaming nostrils, crossing a Lapland river under a moon.

As I pass in the dark through this sleeping town

the only creatures moving on Main Street are moths.
Spinning orbits about the lamps, they fall and die.
Their husks rustle like leaves in the fluorescent light.
Were they flying to Blue Mountain? Am I there?

Driving Out Again at Night

A full moon tilts over the lawns and trees.
Pale shadows, pockets of heat,
couples humped along the riverbanks,
these and the invisible road cure me.
The arc lights are out for miles.
I still carry you inside me, Dad, one hundred
and thirteen extra pounds, gray-faced and weak,
but out here the smell
of water and leaves fills me and pushes you out.
I'm sorry. I love you. But I have to let you go.
So we drive away again
into a few blurred things,
my friend and I,
most of the time not talking.
When cars rush by us they blind me
and I like not seeing. We turn left
over the bridge to come back
and a couple dances across the road, caught
in our beams, the boy raises a brown paper
bag with a bottle in it.
Its mouth flashes.
On my left the river is as clear as a baby's eyes.
When I look off toward the stretches of grass, soaked
   in darkness,
sweeping by, I see myself twenty years ago
lying there with a girl
and pound the dashboard with my fist.
Back in the city
the lights on floor after floor of offices stay on.
Nobody's there. The last
shoppers pause at the frozen bodies, glowing
in store windows, then straggle home.

Lonesome Pine Special

"I was walking out this morning with rambling on my mind."
                    —Sara Carter

There's a curve in the road, and a slow curve in the land,
Outside of Barbourville, Kentucky, on US 25E,
I've always liked
                    each time I've passed it,
Bottom land, river aginst a ridge to the west,
A few farmhouses on each side of the road, some mailboxes
Next to a dirt lane that leads off through the fields.
Each time I'd think
                    How pleasant it must be to live here.

                    ⋆ ⋆ ⋆

In Kingsport, when I was growing up,
Everyone seemed to go to Big Stone Gap, Virginia, up US 23,
All the time.
                    Everyone had an uncle or aunt there,
Or played golf, or traded cars.
They were always going up there
                                        to get married, or get liquor,
Or to get what was owed them
By someone they'd been in the service with.

Lone went up there more often than anyone else did,
Part of his territory for State Farm,
                                        somebody said,
Without much conviction.

When the talk turned to whiskey,
                            and everyone dusted his best lie off,
We all knew, or thought we knew, where Lone went
With his funny walk and broken back
He could hit a golf ball a ton with,

even if he did stand sideways
Like a man hauling a body out of the water,
Being the real owner, we thought, of that gas staion out on
   the Jonesboro highway
You went to the back of
                        for a pint after 10 P.M.,
Lone getting richer and richer until the Moose Lodge
Started to take his business away
                  by doing it legal, and during the daylight.

So Lone went back, we all thought,
To stumping around the golf course, still
Hitting it sideways, still selling whatever he could
To anyone foolish enough to play him and pay him,
Old Lone, slicker than owl oil.

                  * * *

It was all so American,
The picket fence of wrought iron a hundred years old,
Lilacs at every corner of the lawned yard
                              in great heaps and folds,
A white house and wild alfalfa in scattered knots
Between the fence and the cracked sidewalk,
The wind from the Sawtooth Mountains
                  riffling the dust in slow eddies along the street
Near the end of June in Hailey, Idaho,
The house where Pound was born,
                           with its red maple floors
And small windows two blocks from Idaho 75,
Hemingway ten miles on up the same road between two
   evergreens,
Nobody noticing either place
                           as the cars went through town
All night and all day, going north, going south . . .

                  * * *

Another landscape I liked
Was south of Wytheville, Virginia, on US 52
Just short of the Carolina line,

a steel bridge over the New River,
Pasture on both sides of the road and woods on the easy
    slopes,
Big shrubs and trees lining the river banks like fur,
The road and the river both
Angling back toward the Iron Mountains,
The valley bulging out to the east
                                                in a graceful swirl,
The dead chestnut trees like grey candles
Wherever the woods began . . .

What is it about a known landscape
                                        that tends to undo us,
That shuffles and picks us out
For terminal demarcation, the way a field of lupine
Seen in profusion deep in the timber
Suddenly seems to rise like a lavender ground fog
At noon?
            What is it inside the imagination that keeps surprising us
At odd moments
                        when something is given back
We didn't know we had had
In solitude, spontaneously, and with great joy?

                          *   *   *

Today, at midsummer noon, I took the wooden floats
To the Yaak River, the small ones I'd carve from the larch
And cedar chips,
                    and loosed them downstream
To carry my sins away, as the palace guardians did each year
    at this time
in medieval Japan,
Where the river goes under the new bridge
                                                on County 508
And the first homesteaders took up their quarter sections.
From Sam Runyan's to Susie Speed's,
Through white water and rock and the tendrilous shade
Of the tamaracks,
                        out into rubbery blotches of sunlight,

The float's shadows hanging beneath them like odd anchors
Along the pebbled bottom, the river slowing and widening,
The floats at great distances from one another
Past Binder's cabin under the black
                                  of the evergreen-covered dam
And over the falls and gone into foam and next year . . .

                *   *   *

In the world of dirt, each tactile thing
                               repeats the untouchable
In its own way, and in its own time.
Just short of Tyron, North Carolina, on US 176,
Going south down the old Saluda Grade,
                          kudzu has grown up
And over the tops of miles of oak trees and pine trees,
A wall of vines a hundred feet high, or used to be,
Into South Carolina,
That would have gone for a hundred more with the right
   scaffolding,
Rising out of the rock and hard clay in thin, prickly ropes
To snake and thread in daily measurable distances
Over anything still enough long enough,
                          and working its way
Out of the darkness and overhang of its own coils
To break again and again
Into the sunlight, worthless and everywhere,
                          breathing, breathing,
Looking for leverage and a place to climb.

                *   *   *

It's true, I think, as Kenkō says in his *Idleness*,
That all beauty depends upon disappearance,
The bitten edges of things,
                    the gradual sliding away
Into tissue and memory,
                the uncertainty
And dazzling impermanence of days we beg our meanings
   from,
And their frayed loveliness.

Going west out of Kalispell, Montana on US 2,
If you turned off at Kila,
                          and skirted the big slough
Where Doagie Duncan killed three men some seventy years
    ago
After a fight over muskrat hides,
Then turned south toward the timber
                                      and higher ground
On the dirt road to the Flathead Mine,
Past Sundelius' homestead and up toward Brown's Meadows,
Then swung down where the mine road
                          branches right and doubles back,
You'd come through the thinning spruce and fir
And lodgepole pine to the suddenly open hillsides
And deep draws
              of the Hog Heaven country
And start to see what I mean, the bunchgrass and bitterroot
And wild clover flattening under the wind
As you turned from the dirt road,
                          opened the Kansas gate
And began to follow with great care
The overgrown wagon ruts through the blowing field,
                              the huge tamarack snag,
Where the tracks end and the cabin is,
Black in the sunlight's wash and flow
                              just under the hill's crown,
Pulling you down like weight to the front door . . .

The cabin is still sizable, four rooms and the walls made
Of planed lumber inside,
                          the outside chinked with mud
And cement, everything fifty years
Past habitation, the whole structure
                              leaning into the hillside,
Windowless, doorless, and oddly beautiful in its desolation
And attitude, and not like
The cold and isolate misery it must have stood for
When someone lived here, and heard, at night,
This same wind sluicing the jack pines

                          and ruined apple trees
In the orchard, and felt the immensity
Loneliness brings moving under his skin
Like a live thing, and emptiness everywhere like a live thing
Beyond the window's reach and fire's glare . . .

Whoever remembers that best owns all this now.
And after him it belongs to the wind again,
        and the shivering bunchgrass, and the seed cones.

                   * * *

There is so little to say, and so much time to say it in.

Once, in 1955 on an icy road in Sam's Gap, North Carolina,
Going north into Tennessee on US 23,
I spun out on a slick patch
And the car turned once-and-a-half around,
Stopping at last with one front wheel on a rock
                       and the other on air,
Hundreds of feet of air down the mountainside
I backed away from, mortal again
After having left myself
              and returned, having watched myself
Wrench the wheel toward the spin, as I'm doing now,
Stop and shift to reverse, as I'm doing now,
                   and back out on the road
As I entered my arms and fingers again
Calmly, as though I had never left them,
Shift to low, and never question the grace
That had put me there and alive, as I'm doing now . . .

                   * * *

Solo Joe is a good road.
It cuts south-west off Montana 508 above Blacktail Creek,
Crosses the East Fork of the Yaak River
                 and climbs toward Mt. Henry.
Joe was an early prospector
Back in the days when everything came in by pack string
Or didn't come in at all.

                              One spring he shot his pet cat
On the front porch with a rifle between the eyes
As she came through the cabin door.
He later explained she was coming for him
                                        but he got her first.
He drank deer's blood, it was said, and kept to himself,
Though one story has him a gambler later downriver near
   Kalispell.
Nobody lives there now,
But people still placer mine in the summer, and camp out
Illegally on the river bank.
No one knows anything sure about Joe but his first name
And the brown government sign that remembers him.
And that's not so bad, I think.
                         It's a good road, as I say,
And worse things than that will happen to most of us.

                    *   *   *

The road in is always longer than the road out,
Even if it's the same road.
I think I'd like to find one
                           impassable by machine,
A logging road from the early part of the century,
Overgrown and barely detectable.
I'd like it to be in North Carolina,
                            in Henderson County
Between Mt. Pinnacle and Mt. Anne,
An old spur off the main track
The wagons and trucks hauled out on.
Blackberry brambles, and wild raspberry and poison ivy
Everywhere; grown trees between the faint ruts;
Deadfall and windfall and velvety sassafras fans
On both sides . . .
                    It dips downhill and I follow it.
It dips down and it disappears and I follow it.

STOPPING BY THE SIDE
OF THE ROAD

"... as I pull in by the lifeline of the road's white stripe."

Karen Swenson

At Kresge's Diner in Stonefalls, Arkansas

Every night, another customer.
One night it's a state trooper,
the next a truck driver going all the way
to Arlington, Georgia. Tonight
it's only a tourist, a northerner.
I prefer the truck driver.

You can trust a truck driver.
Tourists are effeminate, though good customers.
I hate it most on Thursday night
when that hog who wants me to go all the way
with him comes in; some state trooper!
I'd rather go to bed with a pig, a northerner!

Well, maybe not a northerner.
They do have peculiar ways.
Still, they're good customers.
I think I hate that fat trooper
as much as I hope my truck driver
comes back on Thursday night.

Only three more nights!
How long does it take a good driver—
'course he doesn't have a Buick like the trooper
or a sports car like that northerner—
to cross Georgia? If I didn't have a customer
I'd go all the way

to Georgia after him, all the way!
I bet I could send a message with that northerner.
You know truckers are the safest drivers.
He's not only my favorite customer
but I dream about him at night.
Maybe I could send a telegram with that trooper

but then I hate asking the trooper
for favors 'cause he wants favors on Thursday night.
Still, I wish he was here instead of that northerner.
You can make a life with a truck driver.
I wonder if he would ever take me away
with him. I wish he was my husband instead of my customer!

O maybe this Thursday night that truck driver, my favorite
    customer,
will push aside the trooper and flick ashes at the northerner,
o and maybe he will take me away.

Truck Stop: Minnesota

The waitress looks at my face
as if it were a small tip.
I'm tempted to come back at her
with *java*
but I say *coffee*, politely,
and tell her how I want it.
Her body has the alert sleepiness
of a cat's. Her face
the indecency of a billboard.
She is the America I would like to love.
Sweetheart, the truckers call her.
Honey. Doll.
For each of them, she smiles.
I envy them,
I'm full of lust and good usage,
lost here.
I imagine every man she's left with
has smelled of familiar food,
has peppered her with wild slang
until she was damp and loose.
I do nothing but ask for a check
and drift out into the night air—
let my dreams lift
her tired feet off the ground
into the sweet, inarticulate
democracy beyond my ears—
and keep moving until I'm home
in the middle of my country.

Little America

—FOR FRANK EGLOFF

In Wyoming just west of Peru
there's a place called Little America.
No one lives there. But there's
a Holiday Inn, an oil refinery,
and the largest gas station
west of the Mississippi.
In winter snow-blind truckers
stop there for coffee and diesel.
They might say a few words
about the weather or the price of oil.
Who knows what they might say?
But they'll snap down quarters
on the counter, stretch into their coats,
climb back into the high cabs,
switch on the radio and ride
that rhythm of guitars and lonely women
into the heavy heart of the country.

On summer nights when the sky
is a thicket of stars
and the wind is cool
jackrabbits are drawn to the warmth
of asphalt. They sit on their haunches
and listen to the strange rumbling
of the stars. They stand transfixed
by beams of powerful light.
When the sun comes up
the traveler heading east or west
past Little America sees the highway
littered with their torn bodies,
tufts of fur the color of dry wheat
ruffled by wind.

And further
on the mesa past barbed wire
and the skeleton of a billboard
in the long grass where antelope sleep
a rusted yellow panel truck
stopped still against the clear sky
of Wyoming where years ago
someone slammed the door
and walked away,
with nothing but his father's name
leaving this emblem of something missing
this wind that lays down the grass.

Rosebud

There is a place in Montana where the grass stands up two feet,
Yellow grass, white grass, the wind
On it like locust wings & the same shine.
Facing what I think was south, I could see a broad valley
& river, miles into the valley, that looked black & then trees.
To the west was more prairie, darker
Than where we stood, because the clouds
Covered it; a long shadow, like the edge of rain, racing toward us.
We had been driving all day, & the day before through South
    Dakota
Along the Rosebud, where the Sioux
Are now farmers, & go to school, & look like everyone.
In the reservation town there was a Sioux museum
& 'trading post', some implements inside: a longbow
Of shined wood that lay in its glass case, reflecting light.
The walls were covered with framed photographs,
The Oglala posed in fine dress in front of a few huts,
Some horses nearby: a feeling, even in those photographs
The size of a book, of spaciousness.
I wanted to ask about a Sioux holy man, whose life
I had recently read, & whose vision had gone on hopelessly
Past its time: I believed then that only a great loss
Could make us feel small enough to begin again.
The woman behind the counter
Talked endlessly on; there was no difference I could see
Between us, so I never asked.
                          The place in Montana
Was the *Greasy Grass* where Custer & the Seventh Cavalry fell,
A last important victory for the tribes. We had been driving
All day, hypnotized, & when we got out to enter
The small, flat American tourist center we began to argue.
And later, walking between the dry grass & reading plaques,
My wife made an ironic comment: I believe it hurt the land, not
Intentionally; it was only meant to hold us apart.
Later I read of Benteen & Ross & those who escaped,

But what I felt then was final: lying down, face
Against the warm side of a horse, & feeling the lulls endlessly,
The silences just before death. The place might stand for death,
Every loss rejoined in a wide place;
Or it is rest, as it was after the long drive,
Nothing for miles but grass, a long valley to the south
& living in history. Or it is just a way of living
Gone, like our own, every moment.
Because what I have to do daily & what is done to me
Are a number of small indignities, I have to trust that
Many things we all say to each other are not intentional,
That every indirect word will accumulate
Over the earth, & now, when we may be approaching
Something final, it seems important not to hurt the land.

Interstate

For the one trip of the year
my speedometer readout is cash
shooting feedlots past
where comatose Angus knead muck
rich as their coats, slobbering troughs,
lowing like Israel in Egypt, bearing
that double-golden yoke
of McDonald's. I flip off
pulled up by a Texaco pump,
its hose sucking fresh credit
out of my tank.

Looking around I sense it again.
This side of the road is weird.
A station's red sofa, weathered pale
with old men, their neckskin in flaps,
faces half-mooned by controls
on the Pepsi machine. They watch.
Near Rexall Drugs, the grainsack wives—
lifers welded inside gravel-bitten trucks,
waiting for men who pretend
at gazing deep into windows
of parking meters, their talk
run thin as winter creeks.

Strangers go through as loud riffles
of dust eating this road on money.
It scares. Down the street,
that chalk barn where Christ
is nailed to one wall.
These black coveralls bending up
from under my hood. "Water pump's shot,
block cracked." Staring.
Shifting his grease rag from fist

to fist. Till I admit my check's
no good? As if he knew. And they.
As if for years.
Have known it never was.

At Every Gas Station There Are Mechanics

Around them my cleanliness stinks.
I smell it. And so do they.
I always want to tell them I used to box,
and change tires, and eat heroes.
It is my hands hanging out
of my sleeves like white gloves.
It is what I've not done, and do not know.
If they mention the differential
I pay whatever price. When
they tell me what's wrong beneath my hood
I nod, and become meek.
If they were to say I could not
have my car back, that it was theirs,
I would say thank you, you must be right.
And then I would walk home,
and create an accident.

Filling Station

Oh, but it is dirty!
—this little filling station,
oil-soaked, oil-permeated
to a disturbing, over-all
black translucency.
Be careful with that match!

Father wears a dirty,
oil-soaked monkey suit
that cuts him under the arms,
and several quick and saucy
and greasy sons assist him
(it's a family filling station),
all quite thoroughly dirty.

Do they live in the station?
It has a cement porch
behind the pumps, and on it
a set of crushed and grease-
impregnated wickerwork;
on the wicker sofa
a dirty dog, quite comfy.

Some comic books provide
the only note of color—
of certain color. They lie
upon a big dim doily
draping a taboret
(part of the set), beside
a big hirsute begonia.

Why the extraneous plant?
Why the taboret?
Why, oh why, the doily?
(Embroidered in daisy stitch

with marguerites, I think,
and heavy with gray crochet.)

Somebody embroidered the doily.
Somebody waters the plant,
or oils it, maybe. Somebody
arranges the rows of cans
so that they softly say:
ESSO—SO—SO—SO
to high-strung automobiles.
Somebody loves us all.

Bison and Ass

On the museum prairie,
a balance of preservation and destruction,
tourists in time we gape the buffalo—
the past—
a mean-eyed survival.
Their hunched shoulders are maned
like a molt of old rugs.

Canned in our cars,
safe on our present territory—
a concrete course—
we watch the herd ignore us
swinging bearded heads thrust deep
to the sweet root of prairie grass.
They are our banked barbarity.

Further along, wild asses crowd the pavement,
a compromise of time,
bringing their young for alms—
lump sugar and soda crackers.
They know the score both ways
wild and tame
and the advantage of a soft and liquid eye.

Even half-tame you need
an esthetic eye and stubbornness,
wildness having no advantage beyond itself.

The Stones of My Women

A necklace of women bead my highways
as I pull in by the lifeline of the road's white stripe.

Hilda honey's amber
a ripeness of wheat circling Lincoln.

In Denver Barbara's malachite harrows
opening black earth under grass.

Pat's amethyst is a dark hollow of a shadow
on a slope above Missoula
and further north Ila's garnet embers—
deer blood frozen in snow.

Nita's moonstone is a crystal ball in Carbondale
cloudy with possibilities of light.

I tell the stones of my women
and the lessons they have taught me.

To love the insect kerneled in my resin.
To honor the blade incising the root of growth.
To brave the shadow's hollow.
To believe in the blaze marks of my blood.
To let the light possess the cloud.

Counting their milestones
in the abandoned convent placeboed with mottos
in guest rooms brittle as dried flowers
in motels strident with television
I turn east hauling each sunrise home.

Hard River

I pulled back
the jaundiced curtains
of the room rented
for four weeks in Wichita.
I didn't care
that the only thing I could see
from the window was the highway,
because I would watch the highway
the way I used to watch the river
with a six of beer and nowhere to go
after work, just watch
the cars and trucks
flow on and on, heading home
or to work or nowhere in particular,
knowing out there somewhere
someone was listening to the radio,
the same station I was listening to
with this man talking, just talking
into space, wavelengths over furrows
in the wide stretches of farmland,
knowing no one cares
about what he's saying,
still he talks and syllables and seconds
and dust settle like silt in the open air,
a child asleep across the backseat
of a car, tires throbbing over
slabs of pavement, no spare
in the trunk and two hundred miles
from here to wherever is there
on the hard river that carries them along
and if they're lucky
takes them home.

The Official Frisbee-Chasing Champion Of Colorado

The Navajo word for *unleaded* was not
the most absurd thing on my mind
that arid evening as we rolled
into the fever-colored hills
of Monument Valley: I had been
scaring my five months pregnant wife
with a Reader's Digest real life horror
—a Mormon sedan broke down in the desert,
summer, the whole godfearing family
having to chew melted crayons, tire rubber,
drink each other's piss and finally
slaughter their old chihuahua—
and now, with the fuel tank's *empty* signal
lighting up like a bad cowboy-movie-sunset,
I was sorry for passing Last Chance
This and Last Chance That,
but sorry was not enough, I needed
a minor miracle and I got three:
all of them Navajo and not a one
over eight years old, chasing
a bald truck tire across the highway,
slapping it wobbly as if it were
a sick black goat or a priest caught
buying tequila with last Sunday's tithes.
I hit the brakes and jumped out
onto the twilight asphalt, shouting
—my wife hissed "Be nice!"—shouting
"Over here, I need to show you
something!" The car shuddered slightly
and died. The Navajo kids edged up
suspiciously and why not: I was
the only gringo around and I was tearing
through the back seat mess for a camera,
they probably thought, but what
was to prevent me from swinging around

with a knife and adding three more scalps
to the annals of genocide?
But it was a frisbee I produced,
the old worthless-trinket-trick
with a twist: a whistle behind it
was our old hound who (I lied)
was the unofficial frisbee-chasing
champion of Colorado.
And despite his broken teeth
and hips that shimmied with arthritis
he put on a world-class display,
snatching sand-skimmers, long range bombs,
kicking up his bad legs like a puppy
and fetching that orange disc back to me
like it was a sun he wouldn't let sink
until everyone agreed to make his title
official. Which we did amid much
ceremonious laughter and chatter,
trading names, quick stories,
all the invisible commerce of friendship.
They touched my wife's ripening belly,
pointed to a butte glowing in last light:
"The first people were born up there."
The desert was stealing our shadows
while we talked. I asked my tourist favor:
the oldest said if we pushed the car
a little way, there was a hill
curving down to a Texaco. For thanks
I gave them the frisbee and the young one asked
"Can we keep the dog too?" Was this
how disappointment came into the world,
an easy question chasing a hard answer
into the darkness? The dog sat grinning
with exhaustion, my wife winced
and looked away. Shadows bigger
than any of us were listnening as I knelt
and looked into the boy's black-bean eyes:
"That dog's not worth ten dollars—
he'll die in a year. Let me buy
him back for five." He understood.

A minute later as the car glided downhill
I thought five dollars was cheap
ransom for such a narrow escape
from bitterness. I let out a whoop
and imagined cowboy harmonica music
swelling over the whole fading-to-black scene,
I was that glad.

Rest Stop

The sand grits underfoot on the bathroom floor
below the sign "Water is unsafe for drinking."
People have written their names on brick
under the shaded eaves. Some search for missing daughters.
Russian Olives grow in concrete circles
here in this oasis on the Salt Flats
next to the garbage cans bolted down against the wind.
Tourists walk out to the edge and back
then bathe in the foot bath.
An oil spill leaks out onto the snow-like flat
like a black and white negative.
Here they made the last splices in the wires
joining voices East and West.
There is a telephone booth which stands empty.
Just over there at the curve in the earth
people try to break speed records
at the measured mile, flattest on the planet.
At the top of the ramp a plaque tells
the Donner party passed this way.
So many people have scratched their names
in the plastic cover it is unreadable
but you know from the view
this is country where you don't get a chance
to make a second mistake.
A German tourist stands helplessly with camera
and asks, "What is this place?"
A man in a foreign car with hood up
pulling stuff out of the trunk
looks hopefully at the trucker
passing us all in a sandblast
trying to make up time.

When the Big Blue Light Comes a Whirling up Behind

Leaning back in the white vinyl of your rear-high
Mustang, forest green shining in as big a Saturday sun
as any June day could find,
perfect for opening her out down to the beach
when the big blue light comes a whirling up behind

and pulls you over. The trooper
fills your window. What's the rush, kid?
Let's see your license if you have one.

You fumble it out. Your fingers ache. He lumbers
back to his car, sits under the whirling light
and writes while traffic goes by like planes.
How much is there to write?
Here he comes.

He hands you the ticket and license.
Save your hotshot stuff for the amusement park.
Kid, you drive like that again
you'll never drive again.

He swings out into traffic. You wait
and you wait longer.
Then you start her up,
signal, look,
pull out and stick in the right lane.

Your speedometer won't stay steady.
You try to breathe all the way through yourself.
You would like to tell him
where he can go shine his leather.
You would like a button on your dash
that says WINGS.

A Roadside near Ithaca

Here we picked wild strawberries,
though in my memory we're neither here
nor missing. Or I'd scuff out
by myself at dusk, proud
to be lonely. Now everything's
in bloom along the road at once:
tansy mustard, sow thistle,
fescue, burdock, soapwort,
the mailbox-high day lilies,
splurges of chicory with thin,
ragged, sky-blue flowers.
Or they're one blue the sky
can be, and always, not
varium et mutabile semper,
restless forever. In memory,
though memory eats its banks
like any river, you can carry
by constant revision
some loved thing: a stalk of mullein
shaped like a what's-the-word-for
a tower of terraced bells, that's it,
a carillon! A carillon ringing
its mute changes of pollen into a past
we must be about to enter,
the road's so stained by the yellow
light (same yellow as the tiny
mullein flowers) we shared
when we were imminent.

On Picking and Smelling a Wild Violet
While Wearing Driving Gloves

Eponymous violet dandled in my fingers,
A swatch of violet upon the blackness
Of the thin kangaroo skin dully shining
Where it had fixed the wheel between my fingers
For miles through lowing droves of evening traffic
Stampeded westward from the epicenter
Of meadowlessness to the greening country
On the first Monday after daylight saving,
I lift your violet petals and gold chamber
To my gross nostrils rankling with tobacco
And sniff for any fragrance. At first nothing—
Certainly not the violet of perfume—
Can penetrate the nose of civilization.
A second whiff, and then the faintest sweetness—
The finest elfin essence of distinctive,
Generic airs, the rarest violet gasses—
Comes through, as clear and tiny as a baby's
First word, and reforms my understanding.

Among Blackberries

Off the ocean road in Montauk
blackberries grow conspicuous and wild
as young girls who suspect they'll die soon.
To pick them no excuse is necessary,
there's a narrow path toads leap across
and from it I reach to either side,
taking what I want.
All the snakes are imaginary.
They are the price, here, it seems.
The berries taste so good I sense
some poison,
some middleman gone without,
his children dying of old Porsches.
My hands are stained.

Sometimes I just continue to the beach,
showing the blackberries my mouth
as I pass, tempting them, imagining
if they stretched themselves toward me
it could be said:
they were the beautiful jailbait
who flashed something as I passed,
it wasn't my fault.
There's no easy way, though.
It has taken weeks to memorize the poison ivy,
and sometimes in among the vines
wood ticks climb on to my skin, dig
themselves a place, and will not die.

The Quilt

"He had stopped believing in the goodness of the world."
—Henry James, *The Portrait of a Lady*

I think it is all light at the end; I think it is air.

Those fields we drove past, turning to mud in April,
Those oaks with snow still roosting in them. Towns so small
Their entire economy suffered if a boy, late at night,
Stole the bar's only cue ball.

In one of them you bought an old quilt, which, fraying,
Still seemed to hold the sun, especially in one
Bright corner, made from what they had available in yellow
In 1897. It reminded me of laughter, of you. And some woman
Whose faith in the goodness of the world was
Stubborn, sewed it in. "There now," she might as well
Have said, as if in answer to the snow, which was

Merciless. "There now," she seemed to say, to
Both of us. "Here's this patch of yellow. One field gone
Entirely into light. Good-bye . . . " We had become such artists

At saying good-bye; it made me wince to look at it.
Something at the edge of the mouth, something familiar
That makes the mouth turn down. An adjustment.

It made me wince to have to agree with her there, too,
To say the day itself, the fields, each thread
She had to sew in the poor light of 1897,
Were simply gifts. Because she must be dead by now, &
Anonymous, I think she had a birthmark on her cheek;
I think she disliked Woodrow Wilson & the war;
And if she outlived one dull husband, I think she
Still grew, out of spite & habit, flowers to give away.
If laughter is adult, an adjustment to loss,

I think she could laugh at the worst. When I think of you both,

I think of that one square of light in her quilt,
Of women, stubborn, believing in the goodness of the world.
How next year, driving past this place, which I have seen
For years, & steadily, through the worst weather, when
The black of the Amish buggies makes the snow seem whiter,
I won't even have to look up.
I will wince & agree with you both, & past the farms
Abandoned to moonlight, past one late fire burning beside
A field, the flame rising up against the night
To take its one solitary breath, even I

Will be a believer.

Beer

Driving by, over thirty years later, he remembers the beer. He had stashed it behind a rock in the middle of the river to keep cold. He had taken off his shoes and waded out until he found a big rock—calm water on the lee side, away from the current. Beneath the rock, in a little underwater pocket, a small cushion of sand. He had shoved a bunch of bottles in there—18 or 20—and covered them over with another stone.

And why not stop? He has all day. He's been driving for a week and his back hurts. He turns off the highway onto a dirt road that skirts a field, the same field he passed all those years ago, wild now and thick with brambles. He remembers the spot because he spent his childhood there fishing. He gets out of the car and makes his way to a place only he knows, hidden by trees near water.

The path is overgrown. He navigates by inklings, threading his way through trees, around bushes, until he stands on the riverbank. Rank smell of mud, the soft grinding of insects. He takes off his shoes and rolls up his pants. The water slides over his ankles as he feels the first slimy rocks underfoot. He makes his way to a large gray boulder halfway out that parts the water. Once there, he draws his knees up, takes a single breath, and lets it out.

He reaches in and feels around. Nothing. Then a few small stones. And then— miraculously—a bottle! He stares at it in the sun, the label long since eaten off, the glass smokey and opaque—but whole. He reaches in again and hauls out another. Then searing pain on the third try, a thread of blood on his finger, a flap of skin. Carefully he retrieves the other unbroken ones, making several trips, and spreads them in front of him on the bank.

The Wine of Youth, he thinks, Whoopie! Uncaps a bottle right there, guzzles it, reaches for another. After three he dabbles his feet in the water, grinning. He wades back out, sits down in a waist-high pool and lets the water pass over him. The river drags at his chest, freezes him on the outside as the beer hits his brain. He yells and comes up sizzling with light like a man on fire, plunges wildly back to shore.

He strips, then, and sprawls easily on the grass. The sun is warm. That's when he remembers Cookie Lambert: clear eyes, skin without flaws, flashing white thighs under a cheerleader's skirt. Jesus! Cookie Lambert. He reaches for another beer, downs it in a single gulp. He sees her frolic on the surface of the stream—cartwheels, kip-ups and double somersaults—hair tossed out like a living flame. The sun strikes the water and flattens out, loops one way then the other.

He dives in. The water opens. He hears the rustle of bubbles fly past his ears, feels the current sway, the pressure of the stream on his body. He rolls over on his back and looks up: a sheer membrane of gold, like silk, light passing through it. There it is, he thinks, That's heaven. The water whispers around him. It feels as though his life is gathering in his chest. Still he floats near the bottom, then spreads his arms and rises. When he splits the surface he's laughing, gasping for breath.

Back on the grass, he stretches out again beside his clothes drying in the sun. He grabs another bottle, but sips it slowly this time with a meditative air. Cookie Lambert. What a preposterous name. But Oh Jesus, Cookie, Cookie, he says, though he is unaware of saying it. Now the water sounds different, like time itself washing the rocks. Grass flames around him, each particular stalk bright as a saber. He runs his hands through it, pulls out a leaf and chews it, washing it down with another beer.

He'll find Cookie Lambert. That's all. He fumbles with his clothes, stiff with sunlight and the gray scum of rivers. Somewhere on the road he travels, the road he's been travelling all his life. He's sure of it. Cookie Lambert alive and clear-eyed, hair like fire, who could bend her body backwards in a circle, whose flesh rippled over her bones like water. Easy enough if you looked. Alive somewhere, as he is alive, harboring that body in her body, ready to emerge at a touch.

He stumbles back to his car, clownish in his wrinkled clothes. He starts the engine, lets it roar, kicks up a fume of dust as he rounds the field and enters the highway. It's nearly dusk, late enough for a few sparrows gliding home over the green stillness of trees. Behind him the river darkens, bending inevitably towards night. Soon the rasping of locusts, a few last trickles of song. But what does he care, barreling down the road as far as he can go, until he runs out of beer, or money, or gas, really drunk again for the last time.

The Gas Station

This is before I'd read Nietzsche. Before Kant or Kierkegaard, even
    before Whitman and Yeats.
I don't think there were three words in my head yet. I knew, perhaps,
    that I should suffer,
I can remember I almost cried for this or for that, nothing special,
    nothing to speak of.
Probably I was mad with grief for the loss of my childhood, but I
    wouldn't have known that.
It's dawn. A gas station. Route twenty-two. I remember exactly: route
    twenty-two curved,
there was a squat, striped concrete divider they'd put in after a plague
    of collisions.
The gas station? Texaco, Esso—I don't know. They were just words
    anyway then, just what their signs said.
I wouldn't have understood the first thing about monopoly or
    imperialist or oppression.
It's dawn. It's so late. Even then, when I was never tired, I'm just
    holding on.
Slumped on my friend's shoulder, I watched the relentless, wordless
    misery of the route twenty-two sky
that seems to be filming my face with a grainy oil I keep trying to rub
    off or in.
Why are we here? Because one of my friends, in the men's room over
    there, has blue balls.
He has to jerk off. I don't know what that means, "blue balls," or why
    he has to do that—
it must be important to have to stop here after this long night, but I
    don't ask.
I'm just trying, I think, to keep my head as empty as I can for as long
    as I can.
One of my other friends is asleep. He's so ugly, his mouth hanging,
    slack and wet.
Another—I'll never see this one again—stares from the window as
    though he were frightened.
Here's what we've done. We were in Times Square, a pimp found us,

corralled us, led us somewhere,
down a dark street, another dark street, up dark stairs, dark hall,
    dark apartment,
where his whore, his girl or his wife or his mother for all I know
    dragged herself from her sleep,
propped herself on an elbow, gazed into the dark hall, and agreed,
    for two dollars each, to take care of us.
Take care of us. Some of the words that come through me now
    seem to stay, to hook in.
My friend in the bathroom is taking so long. The filthy sky must
    be starting to lighten.
It took me a long time, too, with the woman, I mean. Did I
    mention that she, the woman, the whore or mother,
was having her time and all she would deign do was to blow us?
    Did I say that? Deign? Blow?
What a joy, though, the idea was in those days. Blown! What a
    thing to tell the next day.
She only deigned, though, no more. She was like a machine.
    When I lift her back to me now,
there's nothing there but that dark, curly head, working, a
    machine, up and down, and now,
Freud, Marx, Fathers, tell me, what am I, doing this, telling this,
    on her, on myself,
hammering it down, cementing it, sealing it in, but a machine,
    too? *Why am I doing this?*
I still haven't read Augustine. I don't understand Chomsky that
    well. Should I?
My friend at last comes back. Maybe the right words were there all
    along. *Complicity. Wonder.*
How pure we were then, before Rimbaud, before Blake. *Grace.*
    Love. Take care of us. Please.

The Cows at Night

The moon was like a full cup tonight,
too heavy, and sank in the mist
soon after dark, leaving for light

faint stars and the silver leaves
of milkweed beside the road,
gleaming before my car.

Yet I like driving at night
in summer and in Vermont:
the brown road through the mist

of mountain-dark, among farms
so quiet, and the roadside willows
opening out where I saw

the cows. Always a shock
to remember them there, those
great breathings close in the dark.

I stopped, taking my flashlight
to the pasture fence. They turned
to me where they lay, sad

and beautiful faces in the dark,
and I counted them—forty
near and far in the pasture,

turning to me, sad and beautiful
like girls very long ago
who were innocent, and sad

because they were innocent,
and beautiful because they were
sad. I switched off my light.

But I did not want to go,
not yet, nor knew what to do
if I should stay, for how

in that great darkness could I explain
anything, anything at all.
I stood by the fence. And then

very gently it began to rain.

Territory of Night

Do you hear
from the road
the horse breathing in
the solitude of empty space,
breathing out through men's initials,
the world branded on ragged sides.

I stop before the black horse
that has been owned and owned again.
Our bodies speak
across illegal borders
of woman and horse
while trains filled with diplomats
rush forward on metal tracks
that will never touch.

There is another language in the dark.
My hands touch the black alphabet of the horse.
The potatoes are alive in the cellar
and covered with eyes.
The dark chickens from South America
huddle near a warm bulb,
the heart of light
emerging from dwelling places
our animal bodies divine.

Fox

Driving fast down the country roads.
To a committee. A class.
When I stop for gas, a highway patrolman tells me
one of my lights is out.
Then he drives off to take up his position
behind a bush at the bottom of the hill
to wait for speeders.

Yesterday, a snake, black & green, coiled
down by the railroad tracks.
His mouth bloody, he moved slowly,
he looked like he was dying.
Boats being pulled up out of the water.
The dog ran into the lake
after the sticks the children threw,
and stood looking back at me from the gold water.

On TV, the faces of the captured Israeli pilots.
Syrian film of Israeli planes crashing,
martial music. The patrolman crouched behind the bush,
the mouth of the snake, hard & red,
his green-black body without ease,
a bent stick by him, as if maybe
a child had beaten him with it, maybe the same
child throwing sticks to the dog in the water.

Hurrying through Wisconsin.
Hundreds of black birds tossed up
from a cornfield, turning away. Arab or Israeli?
The man in the parked patrol car,
the sticks rushing, failing through the air.
County Road Q, Country Road E.
The committee meeting, waiting for me.

The fox! It is a fox! It is a red fox!

I slow up. He is in the road.
I slow. He moves into the grass, but not far.
He doesn't seem that afraid.
Look, look! I say to the white dog behind me.
Look, Snow Dog, a fox! He doesn't see him.
And this fox. What he does now is
go a little further, & turn, & look at me.
I am braked, with the engine running, looking at him.

I say to him, Fox—you Israeli or Arab?
You are red; whose color is that?
Was it you brought blood
to the mouth of the snake? The patrolman
is waiting, the dog standing
in the gold water. Would you
run fetch, what would you
say to my students? He looks at me.

And I say, So go off, leave us, over
the edge of that hill, where we shan't see you.
Go on—as the white she-wolf can't,
who goes up & down, up & down
against her bars all day,
all night maybe.

Be fox for all of us, those in zoos,
in classrooms, those on committees,
neither Assistant Fox nor Associate Fox
but Full Fox, fox with tenure, runner
on any land, owner of nothing, anywhere,
fox beyond all farmers,
fox neither Israeli nor Arab,
fox the color of the fall & the hill.

And you, O fellow with my face,
do this for me; one day
come back to me, to my door,
show me my own crueller face, my face
as it really cruelly is, beyond what

a committee brings out in me, or the woman
I love when I have to leave her.
But no human hand, fox untouched, fox
among the apples & barns. O call out
in your own fox-voice through the air over Wisconsin
that is full of the falling
Arab & Israeli leaves, red, red,
locked together, falling, in spirals, burning . . .

be a realler, cleaner thing,
no snake with a broken body, no bent stick,
no patrolman crouched behind a bush
with bloody mouth, no stick thrown,
no beloved tamed dog in the water . . .

And let us pull up now out of the water
the boats, & call the leaves home
down out of the air, Arab or Israeli;
& you, my real red fox in Wisconsin,
as I let out the clutch and leave you,
you come back that time, be cruel then,
teach me your fox-stink even, more than now, as I
hurry, kind & fragrant, into committee,
& the leaves falling, red, red.
And the fox runs on.

Great Basin Blues

They're having a wonderful time
At the famed Nevada Hotel
Where quarters are only a dime,
While stuck in this rusted shell
Like hara-kiri I stroke
My skinful of poison oak.

The call girls are straight from New York
And the jackpots are pouring like rum
While jackrabbits watch me uncork
On Carrion Mesa, come
Like a signature to an old pass.
Gallons of wine and no gas.

The house dicks never peek,
The ashtrays are flowing with sand;
Eighty-four nights a week
They dance to a big name band:
But here where the sagebrush jerks
Not even the radio works.

Tequilla spills down from the borders.
Bandits and bishops carouse.
A bellboy, enraptured, orders
Orgasms on the house.
They're having a wonderful time
As I funnel my rage into rhyme.

Crystal and gas lights explode
Like supernovae and break
Into bottles beside the road.
Nevada Hotel, I awake
Red-eyed and alone up the line
Under your peeling sign.

Wanting to Be Death Valley

What I mean when I say I want
our love to be like this place is *yes*,
bare, lean as your body dressed
only with want, but also
lush and greedy as my legs:

I would say pickleweed saltbush,
desolation arrowweed, ditch grass
salt flats, briny muck and this mountainous
silence, fat as what we can never say to each other.
I would say *dunes*, with their thick, foreign hips
and geometrical breasts, *earthquake*,
and the air, hot and heavy as that silence.
The salt: pinnacles and pools,
the bad but not poisonous badwaters,
and the utterness,
the complete white of it and the Black
Mountains. *Volcano*, and the intelligence
of roots and leaves, animals that know
how to get water from whatever
is.

We drove across it today, stopped in 120-degree sun,
got out. I tripped on the dunes, wanting
to embrace them, to become them the way
I sometimes do you, lost
my sandals, burned my feet
raw on the sand. My dress flew up,
my bare ass went down into the sand,
burned that pink-quartz hole you love so much,
and I have had sand in my ass all day,
but what I mean is

we could die out here.
We have come anyway, or because of it.
You know, the salt sea floor of this valley

even in its brilliance and stark beauty
becomes familiar after so many miles,
but I am trying to learn how to live here—
I want to send roots down deep as mesquite,
and I want us to come out of this alive,
I want us to become desert.

The truth is this, but also that
the name of this place is Death,
something else I do not understand,
cannot become.

Riding Westward

> "Hence is't, that I am carryed towards the West
> This day, when my Soules forme bends towards the East."
> —John Donne, "Goodfriday, 1613. Riding Westward"

You know that something's not quite right.
Perhaps the town is one of those
which marks its name and elevation
on a water tower stuck up on a hill.
Or maybe the hill itself declares the name
in whitewashed stones set just behind the town.
The big thing is the grain elevators.
The blacktop runs straight into them
just as country roads point to steeples
in Protestant towns along the Rhine.
But these tall towers are filled with wheat,
with corn and oats and rye, not hymns
to the stern father who sends us to the fields
or bids us read his Book before we eat,
who shuts our eyes in calms of beast-like sleep.

This poem is no tract for Jesus.
No fewer evils or epiphanies of joy
rise up here than did in Europe, which these
good farmers left because it was a grave.
Still one wonders. What was all this for,
the grizzled duffer in the John Deere cap asks
as he shuffles to Main Street's secondhand sale.
Rubble of shoes in cardboard boxes. And boots,
old button boots, a pile of iron peaveys
which rolled cottonwoods down from the river,
the forest long since cleared. Cracked photos
of a jackrabbit hunt, the creatures piled high
in heaps before the log-and-sod schoolhouse.

I mean, he asks, as he tweaks his balls
through the hole in his right jean pocket,

why did they do this? What was it for?
The doves perch on a wire above the dusty road.
Swallows sweep into a storefront eave.
A clump of orange lilies closes with the day.
A CB chatters in a parked Ford truck
its back-bed loaded up with bales of hay:
"We got a Kojak with a Kodak takin' pictures
. . . he done a flipflop on the superslab."
The pickup's empty; the owner's in the bar.

The rightest place to worry this thing out
is at the first dead farmhouse outside town.
Sit there on the stoop's blistered boards
as swallows chitter towards their roosts,
the fat sun sinking in reddish pollen haze
beyond the silos, beyond the tassled fields.

from *Cora Fry*

Coming home late from work,
I stopped the car one long thirsty minute
on the hilltop near my father's meadow.

Something plunged and tossed in the center
like a show animal in a lit ring.

He threw his head, he shook it free of air,
his legs flung whichway. There were the antlers,
a forest of spring twigs that rose and dived,
dancing. *Singing*, for all I knew, glassed in.

I rolled my window down
knowing I'd lose him, and I did: he ducked
into nowhere. But I had that one glimpse,

didn't I, of the animal deep in
the animal? Of his freedom flaring

only a quick blink of light? I think spring
must be a crazy water animals drink.

Travelling through the Dark

Travelling through the dark I found a deer
dead on the edge of the Wilson River road.
It is usually best to roll them into the canyon:
that road is narrow; to swerve might make more dead.

By glow of the tail-light I stumbled back of the car
and stood by the heap, a doe, a recent killing;
she had stiffened already, almost cold.
I dragged her off; she was large in the belly.

My fingers touching her side brought me the reason—
her side was warm; her fawn lay there waiting,
alive, still, never to be born.
Beside that mountain road I hesitated.

The car aimed ahead its lowered parking lights;
under the hood purred the steady engine.
I stood in the glare of the warm exhaust turning red;
around our group I could hear the wilderness listen.

I thought hard for us all—my only swerving—
then pushed her over the edge into the river.

Painting by Number

On the way home fom church my land-
locked father would stop the car
and let us run awhile along this hillside
skirting the new graves
that with the last spring rain
took earth and all down
and sucked at our Sunday shoes.
Sometimes we asked him to read us
the names, the numbers of ones
who'd been his patients, maybe
to hear his voice fall back to its
first language, as it sounded
summer evenings when he pointed out
the constellations. There was the farmer
who would come to the front door,
his big face already jaundiced, luminous,
as if death were light inside him.
He'd bring a picture for payment
saying it was his hobby now that he was
dying to paint what he'd never seen.
What he had seen was winter wheat
sickled by hand, and the earth
turned over, black, bordering the river.
Each year his field grew smaller
so that he'd made this other, wave by wave,
covering the numbers, color
by color, until he'd emptied the cardboard
canvas of anything but sky
bearing down on blue, any boat,
the back of a man painted out,
oars wing-tipping the water.

At Slim's River

Past Burwash and the White River delta,
we stopped to read a sign
cracking on its chains in the wind.

I left the car and climbed the grassy bluff,
to a grey cross leaning there
and a name that was peeling away:

"Alexander Clark Fisher.
Born October 1870. Died January 1941."

No weathering sticks from a homestead
remained in that hillside,
no log sill rotting under moss
nor cellar hole filling with rose vines.
Not even the stone ring
of a hunter's fire,
a thin wire flaking in the brush.

Only the red rock piled
to hold the cross, our blue car
standing on the road below,
and a small figure playing there.
The Yukon sunlight warming a land
held long under snow,
and the lake water splashing.

From the narrow bridge in the distance
a windy clatter of iron—
billow of dust on a blind crossing,
but a keen silence behind that wind.

It was June 4, 1973. I was forty-nine.

My ten-year-old daughter
called to me from the road:
she had found a rock to keep,

and I went down.

Poem

There was something I can't bring myself
to mention in the way the light
seemed trapped by the clouds,
the way the road dropped
from pavement to dirt and the land from pine
to scrub—
the red-headed vultures on dead animals,
the hatred of the waitress breaking

a cup and kicking the shards across the café
that looked out on the mountain and on the white smear
of the copper mine that sustained these people.
I claim there was something you wouldn't
have wanted to speak of either,
a sense of some violent treasure
like uranium waiting to be romanced
out of the land . . .

They sat under white umbrellas,
two or three together, elbows on card tables
at the dirt roads leading to the mines,
rising each at his turn to walk
around a while with a sign
announcing they were on strike,
their crystalline and indelible
faces in the hundred-degree
heat like the faces of slaughtered hogs,
and God forgive me,
I pulled to the side of the road and wrote this poem.

HEAD ON

"I am sick of the country, the bloodstained bumpers . . . "
Gerald Stern

The Weather Is Brought to You

It is 64° in Devereaux,
and a volunteer pumper
hoses gas from the expressway.

Troopers with the faces of mandrills
hobnail over crushed metal,
using big flashlights like pointers
in a planetarium.

Sprockets dangle in the weeds,
torn radiators gurgle,

and the dead wait under wool blankets,
expiring
like tungsten filament
in a hissing, broken headlight.

Scenes from a Text

"Several *actual,* potentially and/or really traumatic situations
are depicted on these pages."
—*Transient Personality Reactions to Acute or Special Stress
(Chapter 5)*

Photo I

The car, a '39 Ford,
Lies on its side, windshield smashed
Doors off, bodies strewn, blood, brains
And tow-truck. A boy, perhaps
A girl, rushes about on fire,
And appears to have been so,
Now, for several moments.—Small,
Hairless, and with a face like
Sleep. In his bare, smoking arms
He carries a woman's head.
She is smiling, and her hair
Is all on fire. She too
Appears to be asleep. And the boy
Suddenly presses his head
                down, *hard*
Into her neck,
       twists, and wears the head backwards.

Epistemology

A ripe Indian summer Sunday afternoon in my mom's new shiny
    black
Cutlass Supreme kicking up yellow/red/brown leaves along the
    shoulder
of Highway 1, radio cranked up, after two hours of mostly two-lane
almost at the lake, a perfect day to ponder Hamlet's grave
    anthropology
demystifying the art/shadow duality of his highly evolved fantasies

when she passed us and the guy in front of us and the guy in front of
    him
in her powder blue Mustang convertible—she could have
waited for the stretch of four-lane a quarter mile ahead but she
had somewhere to get to and tried to squeeze in at the last moment
before colliding with the semi, igniting both other cars

and just before we skidded off the road, shaken, but unhurt, I saw
her blonde head severed off on the guard rail roll across the road
into a ditch, articulating brilliantly the mind-body dichotomy
in the still-warm sun, October leaves still smelling like October,
cops striding amid smoldering wreckage through blood running red
    as blood

and without really deciding to, our continuing on, lying silent all day
cursed and blessed in the sun next to the lake that before it was
    dammed
was a stream running between two of my ancestors' houses and past
the drowned cave that's still sacred to the Iroquois, trying to study,
half dozing, feeling the restless current running through our bones

and later, wrapped in blankets, watching the blazing leaves
on the trees reflecting and drifting leaves casting deep shadows
on leaves half sunk in silt, and in the ripening dusk the smoke
of our fire dying down into the sky and the moon floating to the
    surface
of the water like the skull of an ancestor burning to speak.

Accident

Cry of brakes,
a woman splits the windshield
and dangles across the hood like a dog's tongue.

A crowd moves in
to autograph their eyes.
Their eyes stay in my eyes for miles.

Accidents

Smack in the white middle of December
I felt the new car, gray and bulbous
and glossy as a seal, spin on the ice
and ram its luxurious nose into a rail.
Straight ahead, a screen of birches parted
to reveal the cunning sparkle of the river
or maybe, I imagined, shards of glass.
Nothing broke this time. And like the stiff
enduring snow sealing up the valley,
there glowed in the sunless morning an expanse
of minutes, enough of them to keep me guessing
how it might have ended, what other life
might have monitored them.

                    Better, though,
not to think of an ending, but a shifting:
being kicked and shaken into wakefulness
with the pitching anxieties of earthquakes.
Which is ground, which is sky? How different
must I be? Is this what survival means?
One week later, you had your turn. Breaking
an actual wrist and rib in a collision
just north of here, you must have sat and shivered
with the same bad wind, the same good questions.

It's the nature of ice to be darkly honest.
It flashes—white, then black—with the welcoming
half-truth of mirrors, just as smooth and greedy
for our touch, ready to harden the world
against us when we try slipping through.
Each face will end up staring at itself,
each traveler veers off the sleepy path
and runs into the iron-hard persistence
of what's still out there.

                      That percussive instant
might be the double accident of our births,
the merest shrug of time and space apart,
together marking up this countryside
under the intrepid sign of the Ram. Today
let our anniversary be smitten
with a little fear and knowledge, just as the cars
and pale New England roads are mauled and dirtied.
Icy mud spatters the crunched metal
in a revelation: missing us, our death
hurls us back in the tremendous weight
of living, of bodies that can move and hurt.
The supple community of flesh and bone
is renewing itself with every shock—you'll hear
my heart speed up again—as we come skidding
into the world with a gasp, a yell, a crash.

from Cora Fry

I hit the tree
at thirty.
It came toward me
and I saw the bark,
long finger-scratches
down its back.

*

No ambulance
no scrooo-reee   go
get the road clear
for here comes   who

Tom Fox found me
his cruiser slammed
its wheels right up
I hurt the tree

not a word Tom   not
a blessed word
Poor Cora   he
whispered and my

fingers loosened
on the steering
wheel   I bit down
on blood   on his

tinfoil shield   his
tongue going *Poor
Cora   Poor Cora*

Cora Fry
I said.
I do not want to die.
I am not dead.

I only need—
What did he say?
I want to see
him cry.

*

My white gown
parts in back.
No one can see
my devil cleft.
No one will ever
have to touch me
anywhere
again. I'm free.

*

They can
put you back together
but you
see   you come in small parts.
If there's
one missing   some big one
then they send to
Boston   but they might not
have it

. . .

Mother said "Marriage
is like driving a
car. All you can do
is worry about
yourself. You can't stay

wide-awake sober
for somebody else,
or keep him on the
right side of the road."

The neighbors listened
all unvisited
in their quiet beds.

"I make the whole bed,
mother, not my side."

She shook her head, tired.
I have brought her shame—
not that my husband
cheats but that I bruise
so easily.

Who digs her old car
up to its fenders
into an oak tree
and gets dragged out mad,
not even sorry?

"Well, you'll never know
the things I could tell."

"What can you tell me?"

My mother looks down
onto her used breasts.
Her ankles are soft,
her legs lavender.

"Women are boring,
Cora. Every month
they make the same mess.
Every wedding day
sign the same bargain.

We all lie right down
under a ton weight
and then we can't move.
And then we're surprised.
Well, what can you think
but we deserve it?"

On the next bed floats
the lacy remains
of a grand old dame
eaten like a shawl
by famished white moths.
She has their moth-voice.

The farmer's wife nods,
nods in her fat. Hair
decorates her face,
chin whiskers. All wrong,
her signals got mixed,
all wrong. She is her
husband now. He wastes,
still wanting a wife.

We are not boring,
ma. We are just drilled
with imperfections:
holes and moles and eyes

to watch, retreating,
the same backs over
and over. Maybe
the ones who leave us—
husbands, children, cats—
maybe they're the ones
who make me yawn: left
foot in front of right
plodding to freedom.

I'll bet they're even
boring to God who

sees their backs as often
as any ordinary woman.

. . .
Trundling home
from the hospital
lightheaded
gasping in the sun

(Remember
Nan fresh in my arms
sexless in
her yellow blanket
I stood on
this hospital porch
drinking light
with my own new eyes)

Widowed now
by my own fury
buried to the waist
in bad blood

the hinges of my
thighs will rust

The Scarred Girl

All glass may yet be whole
She thinks, it may be put together
From the deep inner flashing of her face.
One moment the windshield held

The countryside, the green
Level fields and the animals,
And these must be restored
To what they were when her brow

Broke into them for nothing, and began
Its sparkling under the gauze.
Though the still, small war for her beauty
Is stitched out of sight and lost,

It is not this field that she thinks of.
It is that her face, buried
And held up inside the slow scars,
Knows how the bright, fractured world

Burns and pulls and weeps
To come together again.
The green meadow lying in fragments
Under the splintered sunlight,

The cattle broken in pieces
By her useless, painful intrusion
Know that her visage contains
The process and hurt of their healing,

The hidden wounds that can
Restore anything, bringing the glass
Of the world together once more,
All as it was when she struck,

All except her. The shattered field
Where they dragged the telescoped car
Off to be pounded to scrap
Waits for her to get up,

For her calm, unimagined face
To emerge from the yards of its wrapping,
Red, raw, mixed-looking but entire,
A new face, an old life,

To confront the pale glass it has dreamed
Made whole and backed with wise silver,
Held in other hands brittle with dread,
A doctor's, a lip-biting nurse's,

Who do not see what she sees
Behind her odd face in the mirror:
The pastures of earth and of heaven
Restored and undamaged, the cattle

Risen out of their jagged graves
To walk in the seamless sunlight
And a newborn countenance
Put upon everything,

Her beauty gone, but to hover
Near for the rest of her life,
And good no nearer, but plainly
In sight, and the only way.

License to Operate a Motor Vehicle

Bourbon boy,
awake old honeybear,
jailbird,
you finally did it right.

Smashed
a car and don't remember,
kidneys
ache, o, that's known well enough.

Where
in all that gauze brain of
yours
is a dry thread? Soaked bandage.

Chinese
poets drank themselves into verse
and you
into jail, trouble, hangovers.

Let
me tell you, tin-man, devourer
of tires;
the race runs tear-ass right through

Your
heart. Drunk patriot salute
that
loose harmony, forget to piss in stupor.

Highway: Michigan

Here from the field's edge we survey
The progress of the jaded. Mile
On mile of traffic from the town
Rides by, for at the end of day
The time of workers is their own.

They jockey for position on
The strip reserved for passing only.
The drivers from production lines
Hold to advantage dearly won.
They toy with death and traffic fines.

Acceleration is their need:
A mania keeps them on the move
Until the toughest nerves are frayed.
They are the prisoners of speed
Who flee in what their hands have made.

The pavement smokes when two cars meet
And steel rips through conflicting steel.
We shiver at the siren's blast.
One driver, pinned beneath the seat,
Escapes from the machine at last.

The Pileup

Waking in the wreckage
stirring again with a kind of life
are faces—black with the moisture
that frets on fenders and rots down
the velvet coachwork. One man
drags a shredded overcoat behind him
fists draped with magnetic tape.

Another thumbs a scorched keyboard.
Another pulls scraps or ruined paperwork
from a glove compartment—and only turns
from his repetition
to face the woman who confronts him.
No recognition. He shambles
back into the pileup.

The freeway is closed now
traffic permanently diverted.
Still—past the signs that say GO BACK
up the rainslick center lane they come
every day now—children of the suburbs
to see their fathers' slack and grim
and automatic faces.

The Wrecker

He hopes
it's only a dead battery
when he answers the radio-dispatched call.
Anyone's day can end in a ditch,
the tow chain and winch strain and buck,
the front end of the car dragged from the culvert.
Sometimes it starts with a scream
then sirens and finally the phone call
to notify the next of kin.
He won't tell you what he's seen
unless you've been in combat, the ulnas
and rocker arms, ribcages split
open like radiators, pages torn from Chilton's
and Gray's Anatomy. Besides, everyone knows
what it's like to be cut by the lid
of a tincan, sheet metal is no different.

He knows the iced-over bridges, the pylons
and embankments, the bad stretches of road.
A kid will put too many miles on the convolutions
of his brain, the tiretread wears thin,
then the mind just blows out at high speed
and he loses control of his life.
When the wrecker arrives the flares burn, red
and yellow lights streaming,
an ambulance pulling away.

Days later the family will ride by
the salvage yard where the savage wrecks
are towed and left, total losses. The guarddog,
a great dane, paces behind the chainlink fencing.
A father stares at the mosaic
of his son's face in a shattered windshield.
The older brother cleans out
the glove compartment, leaves the carnival dice

of graduation tassel that swings
from the rear-view mirror, a talisman
of terror. He will check
to see if his brother died with the radio on.
If there were last words,
then they're scrawled illegibly,
skidmarks across the passing lane
of the highway.

Driving Home

Crossing Idaho the road was potholed ice.
Miles rumbled through our bodies, what vigor
the motel beds had left us shaken loose.
The sky whitened into another sleep.
Our eyes snagged spidery telephone lines
that pulled them toward the buildings
scattered in snow like dice—dark bones
some sucker rolled, loaded to lose.

Over one 50-mile stretch thawed slick
at sleight-of-hand by the owl-gazing sun,
our wheels gambled on the slush. But passing
a Cadillac tight with faces, we fishtailed
blind, swerving like a hooked steelhead,
and tobogganed into the median ditch. Jill
gunned us back up to the road and across
to a stop on the shoulder. Then the Caddy
eased by, dwindling eastward, trivial.

No sounds but Idaho wind; snow grains
teething on metal; the magical, throaty
steadiness of the motor. We breathed.
Our voices quivered like bad connections,
splintering words. Then quiet, we heard
our hearts spinning their blood—gossamer
frail—and held each other till bone
kissed bone through the skin.

Night: Driving the Blizzard

—Near Wayne, Nebraska

No clear landmark, yet I recognize
this: the first faint outskirts of fear.
No change in terrain. Just the suspicion
that the white roadside has gotten
much bolder, is venturing farther out.
Now the first white gap
as the shoulders close in and shut. Abrupt
silence. A break in the tape. No
more information. Just white. I make it
across. But when the dry pavement
resumes, both edges parallel,
and the snow is the same as it had been,
dancing over the road from left to right,
white rhyming with white,
I no longer trust anything.
I know what all kids learn in school,
there is not a single rhyme in the snow,
and every fancy design I see,
each cornice like a fine-sanded mantelpiece
is phony, invented
by the same wind that sends
the flakes slinking over the road,
lets them go slack or makes them fall backwards
and now in one huge gust gives all
the cold careless silks of the air
a toss so that they roll ahead of me,
curling out into gauze lingerie, teasing
along the spine of the road, evolving
into wisps of cirrus, caresses, scarcely
whispered suggestions, phrases
already coming apart into spirits
whirling away as if my headlights
were chasing these shapes

and I've let myself be fascinated again,
I had almost forgotten what I should know,
it is what could keep a man sane,
how exactly this chaos, when not seen whole
but only in glimpses, mimics order
even as the wind combs the snow back
into parallel lines, not real lines
I tell myself, there are no lines in this,
knowing I don't see it all.

Ground Blizzard, Interstate 70

A starved light, lavishing pain
and inch-high torrents of satellite weather
sucking across like cirrus. My brakes
are second and first. From gust
to gust our Ford hood gets lost.

We crawl it back. A blue seed flashes,
develops its plough underneath—safe
but slow as a barn door.
Anne presses her lips. She knows
they've trained me to pass.
The Interstate Escadrille—each hangar
coded Food/Service/Gas. Fellow aces
stoned on mileage, chocolated
hot water, staring 3 feet ahead
sipping nothing but road.
How our neck tendons ache!

Lungs filling with glass, we shuffle
dimpled ice hand over hand
into our crusted 4-door. The snow tires
whine like slow learners trying too hard,
taxiing us up into air getting worse.
To ease right or left my insides
clench, but ditched machines I still
decal to the fuselage. Whiffling
past this yellow Merc our full
fat 50 carries nearly too far.
Out of its slow parallel swerve
my grin cringes back.
Mile after mile our 2 sons doze
in the mirror, Dacron cocoons
not even scared, their windows
a breath of white crows.

Accident in the Snow on the Way to Amadeus

When we went into that spin on the turnpike
  the calm I felt
was pure lucidity—a sense of what was close

and couldn't stop, endless variations
  amid snow-
covered cars; everything white, open.

We'd been doing forty, a speed I'd recommend
  for spinning
on a deserted frozen lake where joy

is feeling powerless, yet safe. The guard rail
  stopped us. I think
we hit it twice, rocked, but didn't flip,

came to rest pointed toward the city
  and *Amadeus.*
Soon we'd be considering mere excellence

versus genius, God's unfair handling
  of genes and gifts.
But for us God was good, or away and unjust

some other place. No longer in control
  or under that illusion,
we drove toward Manhattan like dreamers

in a race for who could go slowest
  in a slow world.
In the play, Mozart is a brilliant fool,

proof of nothing. Salieri a man we've met
  or have been, corrupt,
his work a small pleasure for everyone.

I was happy to be a witness, still for a while
     and moved. Outside
the storm was neither better nor worse.

The streetlights were invisible, though their light
     illuminated the snow,
seemed almost to bring it down.

The Long Drive Home through Heavy Weather

We're caught in the collapse of thunder
tumbling like a slag heap, rain
cutting the road to rags.

Angrily as cats slick tires hiss.
Headlights fix on the highway's vanishing point,
a black clot in the distance that's never nearer.

My father drives by familiar signs: the used car lot's
glare and flags, the Sinclair station's ancient pumps,
the Evening Inn's red neon flares.

The city weeps and blazes behind us.
Ahead hills hunker down on rocky haunches,
and the hidden river fattens like an adder,

slithers over slate slabs, rubs
its swollen bulk against mud banks
and willow stumps. My father chews his lip

and grips the wheel with both hands hard.
I'm lashed to the mast of my own imaginings
as he pilots us past the flashing reefs of guard rails,

run-off roiling over the road's eroded shoulders.
I can't breathe.
The power's out inside my head.

For all I know we're dead,
and this is hell: the two of us
stuck out here in this buckling Chevrolet,

my father's flesh a phosphorescent green
in dashboard light. My tight, fists, knuckled white,
will not let go of the nothing they grasp

even as we take the last curve, turning
into our drive, and coming to rest there, sit
still in the storm's hold, listening

to squalls in the trees and the rain's
innumerable hammers slamming
against the hood, against the flooded ground,

against the infinitely intricate circuits
of our nerves, the blood's dull thunder
thudding in our veins.

The House in the Road

Topping a rise one night on a narrow road
   across country I thought I knew,

I saw I was heading straight to the front
   of a big white clapboard house.

I slapped on the brakes and slowed down in time
   to hold the curve as it dipped away to the left,

ten yards from the front door. I made the turn
   and drove on, remembering that I have done

this same thing at this same place perhaps
   a hundred times in my life,

and that the house has been there longer
   than anyone now alive.

It still surprises me, being there like that,

and for a little while after I pass it
   I wonder how they live there.

Each night, headlights blaze at the windows,
   making furious shadows rake the walls;

tires cry on the curve, recover, and roll on,
   and everyone breathes easy again.

Or else they have been there a long time,
   and nothing has happened; over the years

they have forgotten that every night their being there
   makes someone sweat and wrestle the wheel;

the lights, and the shadows they cast on the walls,
    have come to mean the same thing always.

Someone is driving by, that's all, on his way
    to the town up the road, or beyond;

that I have felt their peril and wished them well
    will never occur to them.

They go about their business, thinking
    no more of cars in the living room

than I, the next time I drive this way,
    will be thinking of a house in the road.

Wife Hits Moose

Sometime around dusk moose lifts
his heavy, primordial jaw, dripping, from pondwater
and, without psychic struggle,
decides the day, for him, is done: time
to go somewhere else. Meanwhile, wife
drives one of those roads that cut straight north,
a highway dividing the forests

not yet fat enough for the paper companies.
This time of year full dark falls
about eight o'clock—pineforest and blacktop
blend. Moose reaches road, fails
to look both ways, steps
deliberately, ponderously . . . Wife
hits moose, hard,

at slight angle (brakes slammed, car
spinning) and moose rolls over hood, antlers—
as if diamond-tipped—scratch windshield, car
damaged: rib-of-moose imprint
on fender, hoof shatters headlight.
Annoyed moose lands on feet and walks away.
Wife is shaken, unhurt, amazed.

—Does moose believe in a Supreme Intelligence?
Speaker does not know.
—Does wife believe in a Supreme Intelligence?
Speaker assumes as much: spiritual intimacies
being between the spirit and the human.
—Does speaker believe in a Supreme Intelligence?
Yes. Thank You.

Turnpike

It was a hole, a leveled, paved, black, white hole
A green hole, a blue hole, grass, sky, billboards, air
And we were in the hole—into the air, trees
Grass . . . into what were the trees, the sky, in us.
And we were in the air, the hole that went through
Itself.
      All around us there was what we were
Passing through, inside, inside, inside ourselves.
And the hole was humming, clear, laned, green and
      paved
With black stripes. And there was nothing, the minutes
Miles when you thought of them, when they made you
      them,
The Buick, the speed, the dead skunks at the skunk-
Crossing, the deer—*I pressed down on the horn,*
My hand became a fist, became a sound, a hole
At the end of my wrist, braked *and the thing was dead.*

            * * *

So, said Death, the deer, sitting there, between us,
With the great, white butterfly—and we were off,
Riding through air, through trees, through grass
        . . . and we were
In the hole, and over the hole, and the hole
Went on forever, into the trees, grass, the sky
That was there, within us, paved, black, white, a rock
A ghost, a Buick-thing, turnpike . . . a token.

Burying an Animal on the Way to New York

Don't flinch when you come across a dead animal lying on the road;
you are being shown the secret of life.
Drive slowly over the brown flesh;
you are helping to bury it.
If you are the last mourner there will be no caress
at all from the crushed limbs
and you will have to slide over the dark spot imagining
the first suffering all by yourself.
Shreds of spirit and little ghost fragments will be spread out
for two miles above the white highway.
Slow down with your radio off and your window open
to hear the twittering as you go by.

Behaving like a Jew

When I got there the dead opossum looked like
an enormous baby sleeping on the road.
It took me only a few seconds—just
seeing him there—with the hole in his back
and the wind blowing through his hair
to get back again into my animal sorrow.
I am sick of the country, the bloodstained
bumpers, the stiff hairs sticking out of the grilles,
the slimy highways, the heavy birds
refusing to move;
I am sick of the spirit of Lindbergh over everything,
that joy in death, that philosophical
understanding of carnage, that
concentration on the species.
—I am going to be unappeased at the opossum's death.
I am going to behave like a Jew
and touch his face, and stare into his eyes,
and pull him off the road.
I am not going to stand in a wet ditch
with the Toyotas and the Chevies passing over me
at sixty miles an hour
and praise the beauty and the balance
and lose myself in the immortal lifestream
when my hands are still a little shaky
from his stiffness and his bulk
and my eyes are still weak and misty
from his round belly and his curved fingers
and his black whiskers and his little dancing feet.

13th & Aloha

Meeting with something of the chaos
and whimsy of a pair of particles,
we caromed, spun, and weren't the same.
I stepped out blinking into instant
celebrity, complete with backdrop
of watery peach, the jittery blue
of early streetlights, gathering
crowds . . . A gathering pool of gas,
ominous—or merely unspooling
its omens into the harmlessness
of a mild summer dusk. Stars rose
to match the glitter crackling
underfoot; there was no moon.

The things that enter your mind,
a vault crisscrossed and scarified
by contrail, birdflight, electrical wire . . .
A scene from the movie I'd been
en route from: how the beautiful
Japanese gangster, mortally wounded,
had taken a comical eternity
to die, false rain and falser blood
blushing his fine white suit until
he shivered, gave up the ghost,
rainwater collecting in pools
at the corners of his eyes:
a moment, a sight worth dying for,

almost. No one was hurt; our cars
were towed, the intersection swept;
folks yawned and shuffled off.
A recollected world—except for one
blank frame, allowing for an unending
series of endings. Last night I woke
to throbbing darkness; fingers fumbled

diamonds from my beard, undid
a button at my throat. "This one's OK . . ."
Visor and badge; glinting wire-rims
in which I saw a farther face, startling,
grave, clearing the trees behind me,
its waxen features rinsed in blood.

Elegy for Michael, a Friend, Killed in His Car

Toward midnight I conjure the intersection:
sparkle of glass in gutters, a fanbelt
snapped, the hosed-off asphalt slick
and rainbowed with oil. Under my shirt,
a groundswell of dark breath . . . *sorrow*
and sleep banded together.
                  And his face
rises, clear as the prose mad Ireland
hurt him into, or the full moon
that followed us home from Nebraska.
The potholed roads rolled thunder
through our bones, shouldered us
toward ditches flooded with shadows. . . .
"One summer I worked on a highway," he said.
"Listen, Joe. It was hard labor. But come
day's end, I could measure my effort:
so many yards of fresh pavement.
Not like this writing business." *Alone*
am I driven, each day before daybreak,
to give my cares utterance. I dream him
bent over his writing table, mourning
its fabulous litter. "You enter a world
and make it real," he said. I almost hear,
on his closed boat's bow, the measured
slap and kiss of the exiling sea,
bearing him toward shores of origins
and silence. . . .
             But my sullen heart's
own noise drowns it out. *Friends*
are lent us, kin lent. All the earth
shall stand empty. Again, the jolt
and weave of our wandering car
on those roads, the bruised moon
low over haunted fields. I believed
he slept in the dashboard glow, slumped

against his door; but the evening's
dishevelled sparkle moved him. "Jaysus,"
said he, "it's a dark world." Now
darker still, and each breath labored,
as the clock's two spectral hands touch,
shine . . . slowly let each other grow dim.

Auto Wreck

Its quick soft silver bell beating, beating,
And down the dark one ruby flare
Pulsing out red light like an artery,
The ambulance at top speed floating down
Past beacons and illuminated clocks
Wings in a heavy curve, dips down,
And brakes speed, entering the crowd.
The doors leap open, emptying light;
Stretchers are laid out, the mangled lifted
And stowed into the little hospital.
Then the bell, breaking the hush, tolls once,
And the ambulance with its terrible cargo
Rocking, slightly rocking, moves away,
As the doors, an afterthought, are closed.

We are deranged, walking among the cops
Who sweep glass and are large and composed.
One is still making notes under the light.
One with a bucket douches ponds of blood
Into the street and gutter.
One hangs lanterns on the wrecks that cling,
Empty husks of locusts, to iron poles.

Our throats were tight as tourniquets,
Our feet were bound with splints, but now,
Like convalescents intimate and gauche,
We speak through sickly smiles and warn
With the stubborn saw of common sense,
The grim joke and the banal resolution.
The traffic moves around with care,
But we remain, touching a wound
That opens to our richest horror.
Already old, the question Who shall die?
Becomes unspoken Who is innocent?
For death in war is done by hands;

Suicide has cause and stillbirth, logic;
And cancer, simple as a flower, blooms.
But this invites the occult mind,
Cancels our physics with a sneer,
And spatters all we know of dénouement
Across the expedient and wicked stones.

DRIVING AS METAPHOR

" . . . we must have crossed some boundary and hardly noticed."

Linda Pastan

Concerning the Transmission

You might say the same of poetry:
you've sunk too much in it
to quit now, driving
good hours after bad
too much of you wound
round the wires and the hoses.

You might stop addressing
this absence beside you,
cursing through the intricate
cities, singing in the high passes,
tooling down freeways,
minding the numbers,
ears pricked for oracular
tappings, limping past fields
of sullen junkers, eyeholes crawling
with nettle and goldenrod.

If you let go now, the bearings
will scream from their orbits,
the rocker arms clang in their cylinders
and the needles return to their various zeroes,
as if your hands had never clenched
this sweaty wheel.

The Drivers

My five-year-old son rides the twelve-volt
   yellow car into the field
of wildflowers, beeps his horn
at the cat who zigzags madly
   before him,
switches on and off the low-density
   lights, turning around
just once to see if I am still
   following.
It doesn't matter, though, he won't
   step on the brake,
won't swerve around the first tier's
   slope, instead goes
over it, out into the fields
   of straight spruce, where,
as he veers in and out of the rows,
it's clear how much he is the driver
   my father was, speeding
to sixty miles an hour at the upstate
   New York winter curves,
the madman who whirled the Golden Eagle
   truck onto Lake George
ice in early April, drove it the entire
length trying to make a perfect figure eight.
The one who never once told me to slow down,
   to go straight,
who gave me two of his last four dollars
   an hour before he died,
blowing wheels of smoke into the yellow
   kitchen air, singing
with Tommy Edwards *Please Love Me Forever*
into the idling engine of the night.

The Driving Lesson

I am teaching my brother to drive.

A swan is broken over the family.

Vast harsh movements of light over the land. The winter
rolls her eyes, making belief. We are small beneath the dry
dream of the sky.

Peter, great tears fall from the planet ahead of us. I hold
my hand up, for I have seen the human thumb drown.

Now my brother makes his appeal in the Parliament of Snows.

How the snowfields shine in the dark! And the farms are little
bright turrets of harvest. We sing as we slide between such presences.

And now an animal breaks his paw at a keyhole. A man shakes
to pieces in front of us. There is something terribly criminal
around us.

We pass on the canal the swan and the snow-blind pilot.

And admit to being a target. For the family begins as something you
drink from, clearly. Then an abbey of black glass. A hotel, veined.
The nose of the family bleeds. Someone is on the roof.

Peter, though they break the swan. Though we are spun out
    *un*lovingly.
The box of flares that rides the waves & will not burn. The glass
of water on the branch. With our feet firmly on the thunder.
Brotherhood, odd chariot, grand tour of the planets, brother good.

Hear it. The soprano of wheat sings in space. Insects in the same
ceiling. *Dear God, time actually undresses us.*

Sitting down, moving. Deciding, we turn here. Queer red shine of the
ice, is it dawn, is it evening. Some frigate, same flesh, some
journey. You listen to my ludicrous insructions. That, and my
other gift for you, this that you turn as you sit beside me,
this wheel, dear brother, this life that comes away in my hands.

The Metaphysical Automobile

I

It's abstract nouns, among the myths of mind,
Make most of the trouble. Where there used to be
Honest chimera and candid hippogriff,
Whom none did the disservice of belief,
We've Communism and Democracy,
Labor and Capital, and others of the kind;
Whole circus tents collapsed, whose shapeless terms
Cover the billow and bulge of fighting forms.

And pronouns, too. I, the erected vowel,
Stands up for a man's own lecherous will,
All right; but You already has become
Ambiguous, while We, They, Us, and Them,
Four partners to a Freudian affair,
Conceal a con game and the threat of war.

II

You can't resolve a contradiction by
Getting between the warring opposites.
The idea of a car either has a dent
In its left front fender or it downright don't,
There's no third way. For on the roads of thought
You're either nominalist or realist,
The only question universals ask
Is is you is or is you ain't my baby?
And mild conceptualists, those innocent
Bystanders, stand to get hit from either side.
Accursed are the compromisers and
The sorry citizens of buffer states,
Nor fish nor flesh nor fowl nor good red herring,
And spued out by the Lamb, the great I Am.

III

In the eternal combustion engine, force
Is from the contradicting opposites,
And yet their warfare passes into play:
The pistons know that up opposes down,
Closed in their cylinders they cannot know
Around, and would not be converted by
The revelation of the wheel. So straight
Flat roads of logic lie about a globe
On which the shortest way between two points
Happens to be a curve. And so do song
And story, winding crank and widdershins,
Still get there first, and poetry remains
Eccentric and odd and riddling and right,
Eternal return of the excluded middle.

Fugue

You see them vanish in their speeding cars,
The many people hastening through the world,
And wonder what they would have done before
This time of time speed distance, random streams
Of molecules hastened by what rising heat?
Was there never a world where people just sat still?

Yet they might be all of them contemplatives
Of a timeless now, drivers and passengers
In the moving cars all facing to the front
Which is the future, which is destiny,
Which is desire and desire's end—
What are they doing but just sitting still?

And still at speed they fly away, as still
As the road paid out beneath them as it flows
Moment by moment into the mirrored past;
They spread in their wake the parading fields of food,
The windowless works where who is making what,
The grey towns where the wishes and the fears are done.

Gleaning

Driving from coast
to coast down looped highways,
I notice how the future
we have been speeding towards for years
is receding behind us.
We must have crossed some boundary

and hardly noticed; people
we once hurried to greet
are standing along the roadside
waving goodbye, your grandfather
in his ancestral cap, my mother
holding aloft a flowered hanky.

Still we continue on,
the car radio playing music
we danced to
how many years ago?
When I try to count
I put myself to sleep.

"Talk to me," you say, "don't
doze off." We must watch for
whatever the stubborn flesh
still offers: the smell of hay
sharp and sweet on the air,
desire—that old song.

Look out the car window.
Hogs have been let loose
in the stubbled fields
like heroes in disguise
to find what grains of corn
are left.

Night Driving

You follow into their dark tips
those two skewed tunnels of light.
Ahead of you, they seem to meet.
When you blink, it is the future.

The Bumper-Sticker

"Yield" says the sign, so you do. The bearded man
nods thank-you, pulls out. "It's never too late
to have a happy childhood" reads his bumper-sticker.
You want to stop him, ask him if he knows how. No one
waits for you at home, so you follow: it could be God
in that Buick, leading you to where you change
the past like tires with a bad grip, or get a quick lube,
the old stuff dripping out murky and dark.

You'd get a new mother first. You'd have the pick
of the lot: she'd be a bright color, green maybe, with safety
belts and such comfort you'd swear she was custom
made. A good, reliable car, never running on empty,
with enough room for the two of you. You'd leave
the garage smiling, head high, motor humming, gears
changing noiselessly, and never look back at the old jalopy
that nearly killed you and broke your back every day.

A new father next. He'd slide into the driver's seat,
teach you the right way to steer, check the rearview often,
stop holding your foot on the brake. He'd pull out
a technicolor map and with a finger like Michael Angelo's
"Adam" he'd show you where to go without getting lost.
No dead-ends, no potholes, a smooth ride my baby,
tell me where you're heading and I'll take you there,
no problem.   The Buick signals left. You follow. You lose
him in a tunnel when a sixteen-wheeler reading "Safeway"
passes you and almost sends you to the wall.

The Roads into the Country

Ran only in one direction, in childhood years—
Into mysterious counties, beyond the farm or the town,
Toward the parish of desire the roads led up or down
Past a thicket of charms, a river of wishing hours,

Till, wrapt in a plenum of undying sun
We heard the tick of air-guns on the hills.
The pheasant stalked by on his gilded heels,
The soft-eyed foxes from the woods looked on,

While hung upon the blue wall of the air
The hawk stared down into a sea of fire,
Where, salamanders in our element,
We ate the summer like a sacrament.

That was another country, and is lost.
The roads lead nowhere. Aloof in his field of fire
The hawk wheels pitiless. Alone, afar,
The skirmishes of childhood hurry past,

Hunting a future that they cannot will.
Children of light, travelling our darkened years
We cannot warn them. Distant, they have no ears
For those they will become. Across a wall

Of terror and innocence we hear the voice,
The air-gun in the land of mock-choice;
Around us not the game of fox and pheasant,
But the gunfire of the real and terrible present.

Running on Empty

As a teenager I would drive Father's
Chevrolet cross-county, given me

reluctantly: "Always keep the tank
half full, boy, half full, ya hear?"

The fuel gauge dipping, dipping
toward Empty, hitting Empty, then

—thrilling—way below Empty,
myself driving cross-county

mile after mile, faster and faster,
all night long, this crazy kid driving

the earth's rolling surface,
against all laws, defying chemistry,

rules, and time, riding on nothing
but fumes, pushing luck harder

than anyone pushed before, the wind
screaming past like the Furies . . .

I stranded myself only once, a white
night with no gas station open, ninety miles

from nowhere. Panicked for a while,
at standstill, myself stalled.

At dawn the car and I both refilled. But,
Father, I am running on empty still.

Rootless

He must have been born with greased feet
to keep sliding so, born at the pinnacle
of a glass hill and then released,

a life spent in the articulation
of hellos and goodbyes. How many times
has he carried boxes through doorways?

The key turns in the ignition, the view
in the rearview mirror repeats itself
and once more his tires caress the road,

their only love. He had hoped to stop this.
He had thought that by buying things
he could hang possessions from his body

like sandbags from a balloon. He had thought
that by acquiring a wife and family
he was at last planting himself, his two feet

sunk knee deep in concrete, but anything
can be packed and his children's heads
peak cunningly from their cartons.

At best he can slow the rate of departure,
not move faster and faster, to take pleasure
in the experienced moment, not the next one,

the potential one. Still, he has often seen,
when returning to visit some place he had
left some years before, the same people

sitting at the same tables in the same cafés,
the same jokes, same love affairs, the same
houses being painted over and over, lives

fixed like stones along a stream, watching
the water chortle by, the same weather,
even the same birds twittering overhead.

Better fashion from his life a boat
with nothing to catch him but time itself,
that distant cataract. Better take with him

only those few possessions he values—
the wing of a sparrow to remind him
of his loyalties, a blue glass marble

to teach him the folly of standing still
and a box of air, pure air, to show him
where he has come from and what lies ahead.

Highway 30

At two in the morning, when the moon
has driven away,
leaving the faint taillight of one star
at the horizon, a light
like moonlight leaks
from broken crates that lie fallen
along the highway, becoming
motels, all-night cafes, and bus stations
with greenhouse windows,
where lone women sit like overturned flowerpots,
crushing the soft, gray petals of old coats.

Looking for You, Barbara

I have been out looking for you,
Barbara, and as I drove around,
the steering wheel turned through my hands
like a clock. The moon
rolled over the rooftops and was gone.

I was dead tired; in my arms
they were rolling the tires inside;
in my legs they were locking the pumps.
Yet what was in me for you
flapped as red in my veins
as banners strung over a car lot.

Then I came home and got drunk.
Where were you? 2 A.M.
is full of slim manikins
waving their furs from black windows.
My bed goes once more around the block,
and my heart keeps on honking its horn.

Truck

With women he felt like a truck,
the one he drove, standard shift,
hammered out fenders, the racket starting up,
heaves of turning over, then lumbering
hard off the steering wheel big as a barrel.

The women who liked him liked him like that.
The one who got him said, you love the drive,
say you do, but hate the echo when you sleep.
It drowns like the whistle of a train.
You've got to come back up,
jump the truck gone mad, that drives itself,
and grab the wheel, take it home, take it home.

XIX

she being Brand

-new;and you
know consequently a
little stiff i was
careful of her and(having

thoroughly oiled the universal
joint tested my gas felt of
her radiator made sure her springs were O.

K.)i went right to it flooded-the-carburetor cranked her

up,slipped the
clutch(and then somehow got into reverse she
kicked what
the hell)next
minute i was back in neutral tried and

again slo-wly;bare,ly nudg.   ing(my

lev-er Right-
oh and her gears being in
A 1 shape passed
from low through
second-in-to-high like
greasedlightning)just as we turned the corner of Divinity

avenue i touched the accelerator and give

her the juice,good

                    (it
was the first ride and believe i we was
happy to see how nice she acted right up to

the last minute coming back down by the Public
Gardens i slammed on
the

internalexpanding
&
externalcontracting
brakes Bothatonce and

brought allofher tremB
-ling
to a:dead.

stand-
;Still)

Jump Cabling

When our cars   touched,
When you lifted the hood   of mine
To see the intimate workings   underneath,
When we were bound   together
By a pulse of pure   energy,
When my car like the   princess
In the tale woke with a   start,
I thought why not ride the rest of the way together?

The Automobile

A man had just married an automobile.

But I mean to say, said his father, that the automobile is not a person because it is something different.

For instance, compare it to your mother. Do you see how it is different from your mother? Somehow it seems wider, doesn't it? And besides, your mother wears her hair differently.

You ought to try to find something in the world that looks like mother.

I have mother, isn't that enough of a thing that looks like mother? Do I have to gather more mothers?

They are all old ladies who do not in the least excite any wish to procreate, said the son.

But you cannot procreate with an automobile, said father.

The son shows father an ignition key. See, here is a special penis which does with the automobile as the man with the woman; and the automobile gives birth to a place far from this place, dropping its puppy miles as it goes.

Does that make me a grandfather? said father.

That makes you where you are when I am far away, said the son.

Father and mother watch an automobile with a *just married* sign on it growing smaller in a road.

Auto Mobile

For the bumps bangs & scratches of
collisive encounters
madam
I through time's ruts and weeds
sought you, metallic, your
stainless steel flivver:
I have banged you, bumped
and scratched, side-swiped,
momocked & begommed you &
your little flivver still
works so well.

Looking for a Rest Area

I've been driving for hours,
it seems like all my life.
The wheel has become familiar,
I turn it

every so often to avoid the end
of my life, but I'm never sure
it doesn't turn me
by its roundness, as women have

by the space inside them.
What I'm looking for
is a rest area, some place where
the old valentine inside my shirt

can stop contriving romances,
where I can climb out of the thing
that has taken me this far
and stretch myself.

It is dusk, Nebraska,
the only bright lights in this entire state
put their fists in my eyes
as they pass me.

Oh, how easily I can be dazzled—
where is the sign
that will free me, if only for moments,
I keep asking.

Fiction

Going south, we watched spring
unroll like a proper novel:
forsythia, dogwood, rose;
bare trees, green lace, full shade.
By the time we arrived in Georgia
the complications were deep.

When we drove back, we read
from back to front. Maroon went wild,
went scarlet, burned once more
and then withdrew into pink,
tentative, still in bud.
I thought if only we could go on
and meet again, shy as strangers,

Internal Combustion

I'm a responsible man, and so
they load me up. Seems they think
I'm a truck with a big engine,
thick tires, strong shock absorbers:
a little gas, some water, battery acid—
they think it keeps me happy.

But it happens I'm also a lamp
with a chimney of glass
and a bellyful of golden spice-oil.
It happens my tongue is a wick,
and when the longing
flames out from my furnace heart,
I speak, and those who listen
burn. Or I don't speak:
I swallow the fire,
and it sinks down writhing
in my scrotum like some demon.

It's that demon who lights my way.
The demon they name if they mention me.
The demon who drives me around in circles,
roaring like hell, eating my own sweet dust.

Journey to the Interior

1

In the long journey out of the self,
There are many detours, washed-out interrupted raw places
Where the shale slides dangerously
And the back wheels hang almost over the edge
At the sudden veering, the moment of turning.
Better to hug close, wary of rubble and falling stones.
The arroyo cracking the road, the wind-bitten buttes, the canyons,
Creeks swollen in midsummer from the flash-flood roaring into
    the narrow valley.
Reeds beaten flat by wind and rain,
Grey from the long winter, burnt at the base in late summer.
—Or the path narrowing,
Winding upward toward the stream with its sharp stones,
The upland of alder and birchtrees,
Through the swamp alive with quicksand,
The way blocked at last by a fallen fir-tree,
The thickets darkening,
The ravines ugly.

2

I remember how it was to drive in gravel,
Watching for dangerous down-hill places, where the wheels
    whined beyond eighty—
When you hit the deep pit at the bottom of the swale,
The trick was to throw the car sideways and charge over the hill,
    full of the throttle.
Grinding up and over the narrow road, spitting and roaring.
A chance? Perhaps. But the road was part of me, and its ditches,
And the dust lay thick on my eyelids,—Who ever wore goggles?—
Always a sharp turn to the left past a barn close to the roadside,
To a scurry of small dogs and a shriek of children,
The highway ribboning out in a straight thrust to the North,

To the sand dunes and fish flies, hanging, thicker than moths,
Dying brightly under the street lights sunk in coarse concrete,
The towns with their high pitted road-crowns and deep gutters,
Their wooden stores of silvery pine and weather-beaten red court-
houses,
An old bridge below with a buckled iron railing, broken by some idiot
plunger;
Underneath, the sluggish water running between weeds, broken
wheels, tires, stones.
And all flows past—
The cemetery with two scrubby trees in the middle of the prairie,
The dead snakes and muskrats, the turtles gasping in the rubble,
The spikey purple bushes in the winding dry creek bed—
The floating hawks, the jackrabbits, the grazing cattle—
I am not moving but they are,
And the sun comes out of a blue cloud over the Tetons,
While, farther away, the heat-lightning flashes.
I rise and fall in the slow sea of a grassy plain,
The wind veering the car slightly to the right,
Whipping the line of white laundry, bending the cottonwoods apart,
The scraggly wind-break of a dusty ranch-house.
I rise and fall, and time folds
Into a long moment;
And I hear the lichen speak,
And the ivy advance with its white lizard feet—
On the shimmering road,
On the dusty detour.

3

I see the flower of all water, above and below me, the never receding,
Moving, unmoving in a parched land, white in the moonlight:
The soul at a still-stand,
At ease after rocking the flesh to sleep,
Petals and reflections of petals mixed on the surface of a glassy pool,
and the waves flattening out when the fishermen drag their nets over
the stones.

In the moment of time when the small drop forms, but does not fall,
I have known the heart of the sun,—

In the dark and light of a dry place,
In a flicker of fire brisked by a dusty wind.
I have heard, in a drip of leaves,
A slight song,
After the midnight cries.
I rehearse myself for this:
The stand at the stretch in the face of death,
Delighting in surface change, the glitter of light on waves,
And I roam elsewhere, my body thinking,
Turning toward the other side of light,
In a tower of wind, a tree idling in air,
Beyond my own echo,
Neither forward nor backward,
Unperplexed, in a place leading nowhere.

As a blind man, lifting a curtain, knows it is morning,
I know this change:
On one side of silence there is no smile;
But when I breathe with the birds,
the spirit of wrath becomes the spirit of blessing,
And the dead begin from their dark to sing in my sleep.

Zeros

Three zeros coming up,
as the odometer turns
toward its new thousand.
Old movies, cars, pushing
2002, the number maybe
we'll get to, maybe we'll
not. As if numbers were
our destination, as if
we weren't close to lost.
As if it didn't matter
how we've already poisoned
the planet, invaded lovers,
born generations of micro-
chips, wired our lives to
suicide bombs, and still
told ourselves, year after
penultimate year, that there
will be survivors, that we'll
be the heroes who'll last.

Tumbleweed

Arms with hands grasping seek to clutch at the prows.
Bodies thrown recklessly in the way are cut aside.
        —William Carlos Williams

This morning the March wind is huge, and there are many of
    them
struggling across the fields, but they travel singly.
They do not know each other. Sometimes one, like a chicken
just beheaded, shudders in a spasm across the road,
gets caught on a bumper, and the car wears it for awhile
like a badge, though it stands for nothing, a poor man's jewelry,
a burr. A fat one, like the architecture
of a small cumulus cloud, hesitates in the right-hand lane,
makes its move. "Hit it!" my son urges. Wind buffets us.
We catch it flush, feel its shrivelled limbs clutch
the bumper and, clinging, travel with us, its weightless anatomy
continuing in a new direction, perpendicular
to the rest of their southern migration
as we forge westward through it, casting guilty glances
north where more of them are bouncing in the distance, bouncing
in place, and we notice, closer, the barbed wire hedge,
how they are plastered to it, stuck, clawing like insects
begging, determined to climb it and to cross
the highway. *Why did the chicken cross the road?* Tourists,
we stare out the window at fields, a roaring tundra
spread-eagled under the force of the sky, at the tumbleweed
endlessly bobbing toward us as if eager for something,
and feel a kind of pity for the dead, who are truly homeless,
at the way the body, when it's shed its soul
is physically driven on, regardless, a bristle of matter. Wind
leans on the car, and we wonder if we, ourselves, aren't
being buffetted across some frigid field as randomly
as these mops of tumbleweed snagged on the barbed-wire
perimeter, shivering there in a row, miles of prisoners
facing the moat they have to get across
as the gods sail by all day, at sixty miles an hour, free.

Nigger Song: An Odyssey

We six pile in, the engine churning ink:
We ride into the night.
Past factories, past graveyards
And the broken eyes of the windows, we ride
Into the grey-green nigger night.

We sweep past excavation sites; the pits
Of gravel gleam like mounds of ice.
Weeds clutch at the wheels;
We laugh and swerve away, veering
Into the black entrails of the earth,
The green smoke sizzling on our tongues . . .

In the nigger night, thick with the smell of cabbages,
Nothing can catch us.
Laughter spills like gin from glasses,
And "yeah" we whisper, "yeah"
We croon, "yeah."

The Commuter's Dream

Every morning an afterdinner-mint
dissolves around us. In it, cars touch,

like tiny hands at a football huddle—
headlights. Rushour pushes through mist

or dark its stubborn, pre-peekaboo path;
a worm fed into a pencil-sharpener.

The Automobile Age

Toward the end, the scare isn't death but life
which had seemed, as we say, a car we drove
or rode in; but now the car—used—
is cannibalized in the auto junk-yard
and hadn't been going anywhere anyway.

Wheels

My brother kept
in a frame on the wall
pictures of every motorcycle, car, truck:
in his rusted out Impala convertible
wearing his cap and gown
waving
in his yellow Barracuda
with a girl leaning into him
waving
on his Honda 350
waving
on his Honda 750 with the boys
holding a beer
waving
in his first rig
wearing a baseball hat backwards
waving
in his Mercury Montego
getting married
waving
in his black LTD
trying to sell real estate
waving
back to driving trucks
a shiny new rig
waving
on his Harley Sportster
with his wife on the back
waving
his son in a car seat
with his own steering wheel
my brother leaning over him
in an old Ford pickup
and they are
waving

holding a wrench a rag
a hose a shammy
waving.

My brother helmetless
rides off on his Harley
waving
my brother's feet
rarely touch the ground—
waving waving
face pressed to the wind
no camera to save him.

Phaëthon

If you're headed southwest, the sun's
Last conflagration sails
Between visor and mirror
Straight to the blood of your eye.
Rabbitbrush bristle like sheep
Against a horizon crossed by real sheep.
Smashed bugs emblazon the sky.
You could rein in your car,
But something guns
Pure energy as if you'd go out
Romantically wailing *More light! More light!*
Till all light fails.

The Road

> We are the dust that rises and
> settles and rises again.
> —SHABAKA

In the car's dream the road offered itself.
That is why we lay down and pressed
our faces into the white line. In the car's dream
the road had just been paved and smelled of tar and paint.
On either side fields sank out of sight
under the weight of the moon
which was full and white and blinded us
so that we had to look away
and into each other's eyes.
That was the moment the road entered us,
winding and unwinding
down the center of our lives.

In the car's dream the road goes on forever.
We kneel by it, we undress
down to the light the moon leaves on our skin.
Then we lie down, our backs flush with the white line,
we stretch out our arms and feel
the road rolling under us, the hills lifting us up.

The road cannot be resisted.
It forces us down
into the ruts, the holes where rain gathers.
Now we know how hungry we always were,
as we fill ourselves with pebbles, with tar and asphalt.
We leave nothing of it.
The white line throbs behind our eyes.
But the road is merciless and forces us on
until our mouths taste of concrete
until our faces are smeared with oil and gasoline.

In the car's dream the road goes on forever.

ON THE BUS

"It rolls around my head as the bus rolls down the road . . . "

David Romtvedt

The Boarding

One of these days under the white
clouds onto the white
lines of the goddamn PED
X-ING I shall be flattened,
and I shall spill my bag of discount
medicines upon the avenue,
and an abruptly materializing bouquet
of bums, retirees, and Mexican
street-gangers will see all what
kinds of diseases are enjoying me
and what kind of underwear and my little
old lady's legs spidery with veins.
So Mr. Young and Lovely Negro Bus
Driver I care exactly this: zero,
that you see these things
now as I fling my shopping
up by your seat, putting
this left-hand foot way up
on the step so this dress rides up,
grabbing this metal pole like
a beam of silver falling down
from Heaven to my aid, thank-you,
hollering, "Watch det my medicine
one second for me will you dolling,
I'm four feet and det's a tall bus
you got and it's hot and I got
every disease they are making
these days, my God, Jesus Christ,
I'm telling you out of my soul."

Enough

The terminal flopped out
around us like a dirty hankie,
surrounded by the future population
of death row in their disguises—high
school truant, bewildered Korean refugee—
we complain that Bus 18 will never arrive,
when it arrives complain what an injury
is this bus again today, venerable
and destined to stall. When it stalls

at 16th and McDowell most of us get out
to eat ourselves alive in a 24-hour diner
that promises not to carry us beyond
this angry dream of grease and the cries
of spoons, that swears our homes
are invisible and we never lived in them,
that a bus hasn't passed here in years.
Sometimes the closest I get to loving

the others is hating all of us
for drinking coffee in this stationary sadness
where nobody's dull venereal joking breaks
into words that say it for the last time,
as if we held in the heavens of our arms
not cherishable things, but only the strength
it takes to leave home and then go back again.

The Flames

In 1972 I crossed Kansas on a bus
with a dog apparently pursued to skinniness
painted on its side, an emblem
not entirely inappropriate, considering
those of us availing ourselves
of its services—tossed
like rattles in a baby's hand,
sleeping the sleep of the ashamed
and the niggardly, crying out
or keeping our counsel as we raced over the land,
flailing at dreams
or lying still. And I awoke to see
the prairie, seized by the cold and the early hour,
continually falling away beside us, and a fire
burning furiously in the dark: a house
posted about by tiny figures—
firemen; and a family
who might have been calling out to God
just then for a witness.

But more than witness, I remember now
something I could only have imagined
that night: the sound of the reins breaking
the bones in the farmer's hands
as the horses reared and flew back into the flames
he wanted to take them away from.
My thoughts are like that,
turning and going back where nothing wants them,
where the door opens and a road
of light falls through it
from behind you and pain
starts to whisper with your voice;
where you stand inside your own absence,
your eyes still smoky from dreaming,

the ruthless iron press
of love and failure making
a speechless church out of your dark
and invisible face.

The Moose

—FOR GRACE BULMER BOWERS

From narrow provinces
of fish and bread and tea,
home of the long tides
where the bay leaves the sea
twice a day and takes
the herrings long rides,

where if the river
enters or retreats
in a wall of brown foam
depends on if it meets
the bay coming in,
the bay not at home;

where, silted red,
sometimes the sun sets
facing a red sea,
and others, veins the flats'
lavender, rich mud
in burning rivulets;

on red, gravelly roads,
down rows of sugar maples,
past clapboard farmhouses
and neat, clapboard churches,
bleached, ridged as clamshells,
past twin silver birches,

through late afternoon
a bus journeys west,
the windshield flashing pink,
pink glancing off of metal,

brushing the dented flank
of blue, beat-up enamel;

down hollows, up rises,
and waits, patient, while
a lone traveller gives
kisses and embraces
to seven relatives
and a collie supervises.

Goodbye to the elms,
to the farm, to the dog.
The bus starts. The light
grows richer; the fog,
shifting, salty, thin,
comes closing in.

Its cold, round crystals
form and slide and settle
in the white hens' feathers,
in gray glazed cabbages,
on the cabbage roses
and lupins like apostles;

the sweet peas cling
to their wet white string
on the whitewashed fences;
bumblebees creep
inside the foxgloves,
and evening commences.

One stop at Bass River.
Then the Economies—
Lower, Middle, Upper;
Five Islands, Five Houses,
where a woman shakes a tablecloth
out after supper.

A pale flickering. Gone.
The Tantramar marshes
and the smell of salt hay.

An iron bridge trembles
and a loose plank rattles
but doesn't give way.

On the left, a red light
swims through the dark:
a ship's port lantern.
Two rubber boots show,
illuminated, solemn.
A dog gives one bark.

A woman climbs in
with two market bags,
brisk, freckled, elderly.
"A grand night. Yes, sir,
all the way to Boston."
She regards us amicably.

Moonlight as we enter
the New Brunswick woods,
hairy, scratchy, splintery;
moonlight and mist
caught in them like lamb's wool
on bushes in a pasture.

The passengers lie back.
Snores. Some long sighs.
A dreamy divagation
begins in the night,
a gentle, auditory,
slow hallucination. . . .

In the creakings and noises,
an old conversation
—not concerning us,
but recognizable, somewhere,
back in the bus:
Grandparents' voices

uninterruptedly
talking, in Eternity:
names being mentioned,
things cleared up finally;
what he said, what she said,
who got pensioned;

deaths, deaths and sicknesses;
the year he remarried;
the year (something) happened.
She died in childbirth.
That was the son lost
when the schooner foundered.

He took to drink. Yes.
She went to the bad.
When Amos began to pray
even in the store and
finally the family had
to put him away.

"Yes . . ." that peculiar
affirmative. "Yes . . ."
A sharp, indrawn breath,
half groan, half acceptance,
that means "Life's like that.
We know *it* (also death)."

Talking the way they talked
in the old featherbed,
peacefully, on and on,
dim lamplight in the hall,
down in the kitchen, the dog
tucked in her shawl.

Now, it's all right now
even to fall asleep
just as on all those nights.
—Suddenly the bus driver
stops with a jolt,
turns off his lights.

A moose has come out of
the impenetrable wood
and stands there, looms, rather,
in the middle of the road.
It approaches; it sniffs at
the bus's hot hood.

Towering, antlerless,
high as a church,
homely as a house
(or, safe as houses).
A man's voice assures us
"Perfectly harmless. . . ."

Some of the passengers
exclaim in whispers,
childishly, softly,
"Sure are big creatures."
"It's awful plain."
"Look! It's a she!"

Taking her time,
she looks the bus over,
grand, otherworldly.
Why, why do we feel
(we all feel) this sweet
sensation of joy?

"Curious creatures,"
says our quiet driver,
rolling his *r*'s.
"Look at that, would you."
Then he shifts gears.
For a moment longer,

by craning backward,
the moose can be seen
on the moonlit macadam;

then there's a dim
smell of moose, an acrid
smell of gasoline.

Winchendon

The bus rocks gently into some town
at 5 p.m. I sort of look at the houses and stores
the way you do from a bus just passing through;
happen to notice
                    a paperboy and his pal
in small-town America
on a forgettable side street back of the hardware store
down from the brick Methodist church—
the friend wobbling his bicycle to go slow,
the paperboy fiddling with the red strap on his sack of
evening news. . . .

What evening news could there be? In Winchendon. . . .
The bus thrums and I'm so okay on it.
The bus thrums and I'm thinking Winesburg, Ohio,
while in Winchendon the paperboy and friend are
already way out of sight,
                            discussing a girl named
Mary Jane,
daughter of Ned of Ned's Used Cars and Parts,
how she says one thing and means the other;
the paperboy thinking of her hair as beauty itself,
conscious that he can't explain this logically.

Up by Ned's, near where some twenty Holsteins
graze stolidly all facing away from the highway,
there's a sign BLIND PERSON
                              and I think "That's me"
and the bus thrums
into gathering dusk
and I ride thinking "gathering dusk"
away from all that other life I meant to think of
in Winchendon:
methods of local survivors —
who's making peanut waffles for dinner,

who's playing Patience over the oil-rag wilderness of the garage,
who's singing "Hit the Road, Jack"
and who's walking fast out to the darkening Common
in the hope of some personal and effective encounter.

On the Greyhound

On the Greyhound from Paducah
to Memphis, a blond woman
asks the driver to stop
so she can call her little boy.
"He may be kinda worried
since his father got all burnt up
in a fire last week and died."
Against the rules we stop
at the Down Home Diner,
wait while the boy is assured
his mother's coming home.
"It was my ex-husband," she says to us,
"so I didn't care, but the boy
kinda worries, you know."
None of us knows, but we hear
and the bus starts up again,
taking us deeper into the foreign
country our country can be.
The landscape is autumn-pale.
Hog farms and white-
shingled houses, billboards
as we're approaching a big town.
If the blond woman were traveling
the Jersey Turnpike, smokestacks
and absence of life
suggestive of some final error,
no doubt she'd wonder
where am I, what caused this.
No doubt someone on that bus
would be talking to himself,
more crazy than different,
too lost in his own world
to be considered regional.
We pass Ripley and Hopewell,

Glimp, Mumford.
The woman is silent now.
All this is familiar to her;
she just wants to get home
to her little boy.
Just outside of Memphis,
a man sitting across from her
leans her way, says "You know,
during Elvis Death Week this year
I never saw it so crowded."
And they talk about the weeping
and from how far the people came.

Before the Credits Appear on the Screen

How smoothly the Greyhound takes
the curves around the mountains,
where trees have grouped themselves,
young and old together,
as if for a parade.

How cleanly the yellow line
divides the Interstate
into coming and going,
the cars rolling
perfectly distanced,
so reasonable you'd swear
some wild-eyed stranger
drunk or mad, would survive
if he stumbled into the road.

Believe, the music begs.
Believe in orderly lives:
milk poured, appointments kept,
beds settling nightly
into familiar shapes.
Believe in the unbruised highway,
the bus that takes curves like a skater,
the silver hounds at its sides
racing toward a town
where it is always summer.

And you believe, until the bus
stops to let someone on or off
and his particular story,
lonely and brutal, begins
with the dark letters of his name.

Bus Trip

All across America children are learning to fly.
On a bus leaving New Hampshire, on a bus
leaving Colorado, I sat next to a child

who had learned how to fly
and she carried her flying clenched
inside both fists. She carried her flying

in a suitcase and in a stuffed dog
made of dirt and the places where she had stood
all night listening to the rain. A child sits

on the roof of a house, she dangles
first one leg, then the other,
as if she were thinking

of how America looks late at night
through the windows of a bus.
From a woman across the aisle, she borrows

a mirror, from a woman in the back
a lipstick. *Keep it*, a voice says.
From a man she takes a cigarette,

which she taps against her thigh.
The man closes his eyes
over her body, such a small body

he could lift it to his mouth
with one hand. In a bathroom she buys a comb
with a quarter borrowed from me

and insists I write down
my name and address so she can return it
from LA or from Chicago or from wherever it is

someone she hasn't met yet is waiting for her.
In the dark of the bus she combs her hair.
And what she says to me is a song

that takes only three minutes
to hear, which I accept
like a stick of gum. *Now you tell me*

the songs you like best,
she says.
And I do.

Love in a Bus

CHICAGO, 1942

It was born in perhaps the Holland Tunnel,
And in New Jersey opened up its eyes,
Discovered its hands in Pennsylvania and
Later the night came.

The moon burned brighter than the dreams of lechers—
Still, they made love halfway to Pittsburgh,
Disturbing the passengers and sometimes themselves.
Her laughter gamboled in the bus like kittens:
He kissed with his cap on, maybe had no hair.
I kept remembering them even beyond Chicago
Where everyone discovered a personal direction.
She went to Omaha; he went south; and I,
Having nothing better, was thinking of chance—
Which has its mouth open in perpetual surprise—
And love. For even though she was a whore
And he a poor devil wearing built-up heels,
Still, love has light which like an early lamp
Or Hesperus, that star, to the simplest object
Lends a magnificent impersonal radiance,
Human, impermanent and permanently good.

Another Bus, Coming Home

The young man leans over
the side of the seat bringing his mouth
close to the singing girl's ear.

"Sounds like y'all having a good time."

No answer.

"Oh, man, why y'all quit singing?"

He leans farther to speak
to the second girl silent
in the window seat.

"Where y'all from?
Y'all from Yakima?
I just come from Yakima. Hell,
that place is dead. Where's
the happening spot in that town?"

Pointing to her seatmate,
the second girl says, "Her place."
And laughs, then, "Oh, Christ,
I brought it on myself, I really
did, brought it on myself."
The young man tries the first girl again.

"What's yer name?"

And again no answer.

"Oh, man, you afraid?
Whatchu afraid of? I won't hurt you."

And to the second girl,

"Tell yer friend I ain't gonna hurt her."

"She's not my friend, she's my sister."

"Yer sister?"

One girl's white, the other's black.
The white one turns, says,
"Yeah, she's adopted." Laughing,
the black one says, "Naw, she's adopted."
Then each gives the other
a kiss on the cheek.
"We sisters."

Hesitations, then

    "Hey, you . . . I mean . . . y'all not . . . ?"

One girl says, "We always kiss each other."
And the other asks, "Don't you kiss your sister?"

The young man retreats to the back
of the bus to drink beer and try
to smoke cigarettes without the driver seeing,
but the bus driver does, and stops him.
And the two girls sing out loud
and laugh all the way to Seattle.

On the Bus Riding to You

"You don't have to make love
to everyone you love," you'd said,
and I'd agreed but now, with you gone,
I wish we had.

The windows rattle, shake loose your absent voice.
It rolls around in my head
as the bus rolls down the road.

"There is a position each of us
is afraid to be put in."

"A friend who has died is closer
to home than one who has simply moved."

All your pregnant sayings.
I write them on a scrap of paper.
The old man next to me leans over
to ask if I am a student. I smile
to think that in my middle thirties
I can look so young. "No," I say,
"I'm just writing." And the man turns
to talk to another old man across the aisle.

"Forty-six years of work,"
the one who spoke to me says,
"I don't begrudge a man what little
good in the end may come to him. . . ."
Both wear wedding bands
tight on swollen fingers
but neither is with his wife.
"I took the Civil Service Exam,
got it all right
and they hired someone else.
Isn't that the way."

His age and way of talking
remind me of your Swedish aunt,
the time she took off her heavy
stockings and you saw her white skin,
whiter than you believed possible,
and you stared—your black eyes,
black hair, Filipino skin.

Once you told me we must all watch
what we say, but especially if our friend
is a poet—for when a poet's your friend,
your every secret may end up written down
for all the world to see. I assured you
no one much reads poems.

You went on, saying, "Just don't
demean me. Don't put me back
in the Philippines or in a nursing home
or all day at a sink washing dishes."
Now I would put you anywhere
but where you are.

I shake my head and return
to my reflection in the window,
the two old men telling their lives,
the bus rolling down the road to you,
making the trees seem to flash as we pass.

Women on a Bus

These sacks of flesh piled in a pile,
Dressed in a dress—this fat grandmother
Makes me think: "*You* were a girl?"
The thin older woman, her mother,
Folds in her lap the legs of a chicken
And looks out with the face of an old man.
You were a woman?
                  Old women and old men,
Approaching each other in life's pilgrimage,
In their neutral corner, their third sex,
Huddle like misers over their bag of life
And look with peasant cunning, peasant suspicion,
At every passer-by, who may be Death.

May I die, not on the day
When it no longer matters that I'm a woman,
But on the day that it no longer matters
That I am human: on that day
When they put into me more than they get out of me.
So I say, in human vanity: have they ever
Got out of me more than they put into me?
May I die on the day the world ends.

The Bus Home

Somewhere on the way back
in the dark between Richmond and Lynchburg,
in the smelly Greyhound air-conditioned chill
slick and stale as cheap hair oil,
a stranger will astonish you,
smiling, spreading his jacket over
your shoulders, your cold upper arms,
as you lie—invisible, you thought—
in the corner of window and rough seat back.

You will know but will not trust for years:
something in your condition touched him.

You will sleep better, warmly. Sleep
is what you need as you are driven
back to what you ran from.

Starting from the Port Authority terminal,
somehow through New Jersey. Then
the long black stretch south
from State Road Delaware with its cafeteria
where you ate lime jello. You roused
at Washington. Between gluey eyelids,
through tinted glass, you glimpsed
the tumescent Capitol and the Monument rising
lime-green, livid as neon beyond
your nearer vision, accidents
of wreckage. Borne on down the road
you doze, happy when you sleep, Fortune's
child. Doomed one, blessed one. Not
till you have finished failing may you prophesy.

Upstate

A knife blade of cold air keeps prying
the bus window open. The spring country
won't be shut out. The door to the john
keeps banging. There're a few of us:
a stale-drunk or stoned woman in torn jeans,
a Spanish-American salesman, and, ahead,
a black woman folded in an overcoat.
Emptiness makes a companionable aura
through the upstate villages—repetitive,
but crucial in their little differences
of fields, wide yards with washing, old machinery—where people live
with the highway's patience and flat certainty.

Sometimes I feel sometimes
the Muse is leaving, the Muse is leaving America.
Her tired face is tired of iron fields,
its hollows sing the mines of Appalachia,
she is a chalk-thin miner's wife with knobbled elbows,
her neck tendons taut as banjo strings,
she who was once a freckled palomino with a girl's mane
galloping blue pastures plinkety-plunkety,
staring down at a tree-stunned summer lake,
when all the corny calendars were true.
The departure comes over me in smoke
from the far factories.

But were the willows lyres, the fanned-out pollard willows
with clear translation of water into song,
were the starlings as heartbroken as nightingales,
whose sorrow piles the looming thunderhead
over the Catskills, what would be their theme?
The spring hills are sun-freckled, the chaste white barns flash
through screening trees the vigor of her dream,
like a white plank bridge over a quarreling brook.
Clear images! Direct as your daughters

in the way their clear look returns your stare,
unarguable and fatal—
no, it is more sensual.
I am falling in love with America.

I must put the cold small pebbles from the spring
upon my tongue to learn her language,
to talk like birch or aspen confidently.
I will knock at the widowed door
of one of these villages
where she will admit me like a broad meadow,
like a blue space between mountains,
and holding her arms at the broken elbows
brush the dank hair from a forehead
as warm as bread or as a homecoming.

Passing Through

"I think a dream of darkness kept me going . . ."

John Calderazzo

Passing through Barre

A small town at the end of autumn,
pickups weathered hubdeep in leaves,
a stock car raised on blocks
with a bunch of dried flowers
stuffed in the radiator,

the local dropouts lounging
on the steps of Town Hall (now closed,
black shutters scrubbed and sealed)

act a double feature
the soundtrack of which only
they can hear, cruel afternoons
on Friday, the cold coming back
colder, precise, badly usual,
quicker than the jackknife
you never see,

and the library across from the green,
closed too, with its three books
slowly cracking their fragile spines
on shelves
in the unvisited dark.

The Blond Road

This road dips and climbs but never bends.
The line it finally is strings far beyond
my sight, still the color of useless dirt.
Trees are a hundred greens in varying light
as sky breaks black on silver over and in
the sea. Not one home or car. No shacks
abandoned to the storms. On one side,
miles of high grass; on the other, weather
and the sea reflecting tons of a wild day.

The wind is from Malay. Tigers in the wind
make lovers claw each other orange. Blond
dirt rises to recite the lies of summer
before the wind goes north and cats rip
white holes in the sky. Fields are grim
and birds along this road are always stone.

I planned to cheat the road with laughter.
Build a home no storm could crack
and sing my Fridays over centuries of water—
once more, have me back, my awkward weather—
but the land is not for sale. Centuries
are strung: a blond road north and south
and no man will improve it with macadam.

The road is greased by wind. Sun has turned
the blond dirt brown, the brown grass
black and dark ideas of the ocean
silver. Each month rolls along the road
with an hour's effort. Now the lovers
can't recall each other or identify
that roar: the northern pain of tigers.

I know that just a word I'll never have
could make the brown road blond again
and send the stone birds climbing to their names.

Red Twilight

I got caught in the wrong lane last night,
Driving home from work, and tried
To turn left against traffic,
And entered the dusk and molasses
Of Halloween. It was Halloween,

And I had decided to seek a healthfood store
East of here to buy brewer's yeast
To help keep a grip on my nerves.
I needed yeast, nutritional yeast,
Which smells like feet,

Discourages fleas and mosquitos
As a bonus effect, makes things rise
Like hope and hair, and keeps things low.
Then an asshole in a Toyota
Tooted to criticize my driving

And prevent my entering his lane,
And after a minute of chicken jockeying
And waste of gas, I allowed his point
And we exchanged signs to say goodbye,
Finger gestures. Then I lost my way,

Driving east where the last of day
Was the rose of a dog's mouth, black
At its crust and core as mold. I was
New to this town. One false move
And all I understood was gone.

The asshole turned off at a housing
Project. I had my tire wrench at hand,
But didn't follow him into his lot
To say, "You must be miserable. Well,
I am miserable too. Take a swing

At my head with this tire iron. We'll see
If I can stagger after you, my interest
Being in crushing your larynx."
But I drove lost, drove mute,
Into the engrossing twilight,

Black water, pink moss, got on
The interstate, got off
And faced a firing squad
Of directional arrows saying,
Don't enter here, oneway,

Go back, stop. I passed a path
Barred by a snake of cable
Anchored to iron holes in the noses
Of concrete pyramids to block locals
from dumping construction debris.

I took a road running past
A yellow bungalow, an empty drive
Where I pulled in to turn around.
Cardboard cartons collapsed by rain
Sat huddled under a sumac. Someone

Had run away from life a failure,
Then got evicted later. What
I could see peeking out
Of the rotten boxes was all
Pastel: blankets, plastic

Kitchen gear, toys. I was near
The reservation, what's called
The Onondaga Nation. I returned
To the bypass, the road home,
The teepee where I make peepee,

Car aimed at ultimate Buffalo,
And the mother of all redness,
The west. The sky was the earth's dress

And lice like us were loose in its
Furrows with bloodspot taillights,

Framed by bushes of leafless trees.
An army of corpuscle stars
Came out and stood whispering,
"We're fresh and cool and white,
Let's dance." It was late Halloween

In North America, and I had not
Forgotten Nicolai Ceauşescu,
The great murderer of Rumania,
How the citizens rose up,
And caught him and shot him,

And likewise Elena, his wife,
Whose hands they had tied
And who wouldn't stop blubbering:
Trick or treat, Mrs. Ceauşescu.
Thank you, and good night. You see,

I tried to turn left against traffic
And got lost, a family, a century
Got lost, my grandparents, so
Full of anger and pity, peasants
And children of peasants like me.

Recurring Highway

One of the passengers beside me shook his head: "I can
hear the last symphony, that's what I've been trained
for. Like all music, very sad and very beautiful. The
small talk frightens me, great events flash by . . ."

Driving home, the long flat prairie at night. I could see
certain fires and lamps, but it was impossible to deter-
mine their size or distance against the depthless black
empty space. Ten thousand years on the edge of a
cliff, without time for a guided tour, without birthdays
or deadlines.

Dream of Darkness

Down from the Black Hills, heading home,
we drove and drove through South Dakota.

The sun was spiked to the sky,
but its heat rolled on like a boulder

flattening farms and miles of grass,
pushing knives into the cracked prairie.

When the hills began to glow like coals
we wrapped ourselves with dripping towels.

You kept melting in your seat,
but I did not.

I think a dream of darkness kept me going.
I felt it leap from deep within me

and race beyond the day
into dusk and the cool bloom of the stars.

And so, driving on, I inhaled the constellations
and let a stony moon beat down.

I made a small wind trickle through my bones.
I even shivered while the heat rolled on.

Morning Harvest

> Pennsylvania spiders
not only stretch their silk between the limbs
of our great trees but hang between our houses
and pull their sheets across the frantic eyes
of cats and the soft chests of men.
Some are so huge they move around like mammals,
waddling slowly over the rough cement
and into the bushes to nurse their young or feed
on berries and crunch on bones.
But it is the ones that live on the iron bridge
going across to Riegelsville, New Jersey,
that are the most artistic and luxurious.
They make their webs between the iron uprights
and hang them out in the dew above the river
like a series of new designs on display,
waiting for you to choose the one most delicate,
waiting for you to touch the sticky threads
as you look at their soft silk, as you love them.

If your mind is already on business,
even if your mind is still into your dream,
you will be shocked by their beauty and you will sit there
two minutes, two hours, a half a century you will sit there
until the guards begin to shout, until they rush up in confusion
and bang on your window and look at you in fear.
You will point with your left finger at the sun
and draw a tracery in the cold air,
a dragline from door handle to door handle,
foundation lines inside the windows,
long radials from the panel to the headrest
and gluey spirals turning on the radials;
and you will sit in the center of your web
like a rolled-up leaf or a piece of silent dirt,
pulling gently on your loose trapline.
They will scream in your ear,

they will tear desperately at the sheets,
they will beg for air
before you finally relieve them by starting your engine
and moving reluctantly over the small bridge.

Do not regret your little bout with life in the morning.
If you drive slowly you can have almost one minute
to study the drops of silver hanging in the sun
before you turn the corner past the gatehouse
and down the road beside the railroad cars
and finally over the tracks and up the hill
to the morning that lies in front of you like one more design.
It is the morning I live in and travel through,
the morning of children standing in the driveways,
of mothers wrapping their quilted coats around them
and yellow buses flashing their lights like berserk police cars.
It is lights that save us, lights that light the way,
blue lights rushing in to help the wretched,
red lights carrying twenty pounds of oxygen down the highway,
white lights entering the old Phoenician channels
bringing language and mathematics and religion into the darkness.

Crossing the Desert

Little animals call
us, tiny feet whisper, and
a certain wide wing shadow
flickers down the gray wind
over the sage.

Pardon! Pardon!—
a ditch at night is a church
where eyes burn candles, mile after
silent mile, whatever comes,
whatever comes.

Every time the world comes
true, they cry from the ditch,
our cousins offering their paws,
a light hanging in their eyes,
returning our own.

Snow On The Desert

"Each ray of sunshine is seven minutes old,"
Serge told me in New York one December night.

"So when I look at the sky, I see the past?"
"Yes, Yes," he said, "especially on a clear day."

On January 19, 1987,
as I very early in the morning
drove my sister to Tucson International,

suddenly on Alvernon and 22nd Street
the sliding doors of the fog were opened,

and the snow, which had fallen all night, now
sun-dazzled, blinded us, the earth whitened

out, as if by cocaine, the desert's plants,
its mineral-hard colors extinguished,
wine frozen in the veins of the cactus.

* * *

The Desert Smells Like Rain: in it I read:
The syrup from which sacred wine is made

is extracted from the saguaros each
summer. The Papagos place it in jars,

where the last of it softens, then darkens
into a color of blood though it tastes

strangely sweet, almost white, like a dry wine.
As I tell Sameetah this, we are still

seven miles away. "And you know the flowers
of the saguaros bloom only at night?"

We are driving slowly, the road is glass.
"Imagine where we are was a sea once.

Just imagine!" The sky is relentlessly
sapphire, and the past is happening quickly:

the saguaros have opened themselves, stretched
out their arms to rays millions of years old,

in each ray a secret of the planet's
origin, the rays hurting each cactus

into memory, a human memory—
for they are human, the Papagos say:

not only because they have arms and veins
and secrets. But because they too are a tribe,

vulnerable to massacre. "It is like
the end, perhaps the beginning of the world,"

Sameetah says, staring at their snow-sleeved
arms. And we are driving by the ocean

that evaporated here, by its shores,
the past now happening so quickly that each

stop light hurts us into memory, the sky
taking rapid notes on us as we turn

at Tucson Boulevard and drive into
the airport, and I realize that the earth

is thawing from longing into longing and
that we are being forgotten by those arms.

* * *

At the airport I stared after her plane

till the window was

                again a mirror.
As I drove back to the foothills, the fog

shut its doors behind me on Alvernon,
and I breathed the dried seas

                the earth had lost,
their forsaken shores. And I remembered

another moment that refers only
to itself:

                in New Delhi one night
as Begum Akhtar sang, the lights went out.

It was perhaps during the Bangladesh War,
perhaps there were sirens,

                air-raid warnings.
But the audience, hushed, did not stir.

The microphone was dead, but she went on
singing, and her voice

                was coming from far
away, as if she had already died.

And just before the lights did flood her
again, melting the frost

                of her diamond
into rays, it was, like this turning dark

of fog, a moment when only a lost sea
can be heard, a time

                to recollect
every shadow, everything the earth was losing,

a time to think of everything the earth
and I had lost, of all

                  that I would lose,
of all that I was losing.

Cross-Country, & Motif Appears

1.

The Volks grows close as a skullcap.
Forty hours—by 11 p.m. near Chittenango
we lose Brook Benton's voice, and static
scratches like a rat to be let from the radio.
We alternate; the wheel marries us
surer than a ring, black sky's our rabbi. Night

vision; retinas, like personal ravens
through portholes, leave our eyes and return
with no twig of destination. Whatever
belief is, it's something to do with the world passing
hazily into morning, sky the color of vichyssoise, and everything
following the centerline like it mattered. Day

means a black pine likened by snow
to a nun, means snow blown moire across blacktop.
Noon means it melts and we're that much closer.
The windshield wiper streaks a slush/dirt arch this
light rainbows fitfully in: a small god, a
small sign of covenant.

2. "*Lord, I believe it's rainin' all over the world.*"
        —as sung by Brook Benton

The road makes everything road. Makes
eyes: a tunnel, road spools into; makes hands
on the wheel: hilled landscape, road cuts. I
look at you (it blurs the world out of the window) for
something . . . a human moue: pout, smile, your own goony
eyes crossed for laughs, or for luck. For luck

we knuckle wood, fling salt, rice, douche in
such-and-soforth solution, kneel

to gods' bodies or who's handy, wish on
candle and bone, beg star. In Anatolia,
at Ararat, they climbed the mountain up
17,000 ice-like-knives feet—for luck,

for relics, pitchy splinters hatcheted from The Ark some
said really rested there glacier-wedged. So
they trudged it, by rope, with pick, and held on
sometimes by no more than thumbnail-width to a cliffwall,
suspended. And so I think of them, for
luck, also clinging to a face.

What I See When I Drive To Work

(BOSTON TO NEW YORK)

On clear days it's fast black dead west sixty miles,
New England blazing or granite-brown
on both sides of the slide. Then a dip south-
west—the sun on my left cheek now flat
on my chest, and I'm warm,
with the other citizens, driving
to work. About lunchtime

I hit Hartford (each week a honk
for Wallace Stevens)—half a day done
for the insurance clerks and I'm halfway
to work. Twenty or so miles later,
on the arc of a long dropping curve, the sun
takes a quarry's gouged-out bowl.
I like the big machines, drills

and dozers, that eat
the rock and break it down to sand—at least
more than I like the insurance industry;
and then a town's announced
by a giant Jesus' coat rack
on a rubbled hill. It overlooks
a happy, placid burg known for brass

where I never stop
for gas or sandwich. I'm driving
to work—talk radio/gun control, Squantz
Pond, lunch pail, Ruby Road, never-cross-
a-picket-line, on my way
to earn a wage: Massachusetts, Connecticut,
and now nudging into New York,

just over which border

I follow for a few miles a river
that opens to a lake
that each day this fall
is open to more and more ducks,
which makes me happy, at this point,
driving to work with the rest of America,

who mostly get there before I do.
The last leg's most scenic, woodsy,
and takes me past a publishing complex,
Reader's Digest, Inc., massive buidings
on a hill, where a man someday
might reduce this poem to a haiku.
I'm nearing now and exit by the exit

by the blind school—two more miles,
if I take the shortcut past some mansions,
to my office, which is
199.4 mi.
from my home. It's a lengthy motoring,
but the work is honest
and the customers human.

On The Way To Work

> Life is a bitch. And then you die.
> —a bumper sticker

I hated bumper stickers, hated
the notion of wanting to be known
by one glib or earnest thing.
But this time I sped up to see
a woman in her forties, cigarette,
no way to tell how serious
she was, to what degree she felt
the joke, or what she wanted from us
who'd see it, philosophers all.
If I'd had my own public answer—
"New Hope For The Dead,"
the only sticker I almost stuck—
I would have driven in front of her
and slowed down. How could we not
have become friends
or the kind of enemies
who must talk into the night,
just one mistake away from love?
I rode parallel to her,
glancing over, as one does
on an airplane at someone's book.
Short, straight hair. No make-up.
A face that had been a few places
and only come back from some.
At the stop light I smiled
at her, then made my turn
toward the half-life of work
past the placebo shops
and the beautiful park, white
like a smokescreen with snow.
She didn't follow, not in this
bitch of a life.
And I had so much to tell her

before we die
about what I'd done all these years
in between, under, and around
truths like hers. Who knows
where we would have stopped?

Merge

The Midtown Tunnel is a car sewer.
It winds your watch until it squirts.
You want to bite your knees,

strangle your steering wheel, buzz
in neutral, flip stations, blip all buttons.
Your highway taxes at work. Squeeze

right. You're all by your
lonesome everyone else's. O yield Brother,
yield. And merge.

A Drive in the Country

In the ditch by the dirt back road
late in March, a few black snowdrifts
lie in the grass like old men
asleep in their coats. It's the dirt
of the road that has kept them
so cold at the heart. We drive by
without stopping for them.

Smiling at 180

You hold it floored, between 90/95
never passing the North Platte,
glimpsing where its gone waters stumbled
and graveled among
a rubbage of mudbark willow.

Crows flapping the bare clod fields
in low gusts.
The black road flapping your tires.
The winter sun in husks.

There was a sea here once.

The slow Nebraska prairie heaves
its thick troughs and swells,
shouldering past into a rear view
at the base of your skull.

Suddenly out of the other direction
the right girl comes along fast
barrcling her red Camaro—
a friend's sock feet
up and sleeping in back.

You each flick a smile forever
at 180
and split wide open
into a small pair of mirrors.

Car Radio

An in-joke and the long days faltering
at the edge of fields just visible as we
drive on, the windows shuddering in twilight,
are parts of the songs. And we are travelling
faster all the time, no way to keep
up with them. Between ourselves and the night
coming on to uneasy towns like smoke
the songs are a commitment we do not make
that gets made for us. Our own words reshaped
into the reliable, broken speech of the next
town and all those after it. As we
drive on, we see each one of them escape
us, certain that it will reappear in the context
of another song, the in-joke of the whole country.

An Introduction to New Jersey

> The Eskimo has fifty words for snow.
> —an anthropological truism

Consider our gentler tundra,
say U.S. 3 West, near midnight,
the slow, spiralling climb
out of Lincoln Tunnel—
how as you rise the whole
midtown skyline rises with you
like a wall of lighted newsprint
while columns of headlights
floating queasily somehow hold
formation, though every driver's
drunk—how the viaduct
finally slings all lanes off
strict west toward Secaucus,
Newark, Delaware Water Gap,
side by side at seventy,
the Empire State a lighted target
fastened to your back while
all about you flakes of light
fly faster, the news grows thicker,
pages of it coming up behind
you, turning in the mirror—
how I still, by heart, remember
where certain lanes for no
apparent reason peter out.
There's help in Montclair,
I would say, handing my car keys
to the Eskimo, knowing
he wouldn't live five minutes
out there.

Coming Home, Garden State Parkway

Tonight the toll booth men are
congratulating the weather,
wishing me well. I'm all thank you's
and confusion, I don't know what

kind of conspiracy this is.
Then at Howard Johnson's
the pretty cashier apologizes
for the price of coffee. She wants me

to drive carefully, to think of her
on the dark, straight road.
Does she say these things to everyone?
I've done nothing different

and in the mirror
there's the same old face
not even lovers have called handsome,
the same mouth that belies

absolute conviction.
I'm alone, and maybe
there's an underworld of those alone
and maybe tonight I've entered it—

the instant, safe intimacy
guaranteed to move on.
On the car radio
comes a noisy current song

and then an old, melodic lie
about love.
Afterwards, the disc jockey
speaks to all of us on the road,

he wants us to understand
the danger of the other man,
watch out, he says, for the blind side.
I'm going 70, the winter outside

is without snow, it's hard anymore
to be sure about anything.
Next toll station, I feel for a quarter—
the exact change

but I swerve
(as I knew I would)
to the woman holding out her hand.
She neither smiles nor speaks,

I try to believe
she's shy.
I'd like to put my hand in her hand,
to keep alive

this strange human streak I'm on.
But there's only money between us,
silver and flesh
meeting in a familiar goodbye.

Driving the Coeur d'Alene without You

Rain shadows the lake,
and the road curves away and then back,
back and then up, and the sun
appears and disappears.

Below,
the knifetip flash and white wing-dip of mainsails,
the blue of sunburst spinnakers.

In a green fjord,
a canopied motor launch turns the water back
in two icy curls from its prow.

I tell you,
the dumb stain on my shirtpocket
could pass for loneliness.

I want it over quickly.

One by one,
the bays go by: Beauty, Turner, Bell . . .
and long,
dusty constellations of mountain asters.

At Powderhorn,
I pass a family of three
picking berries.

The woman
a print dress in the brambles.
The man hardly glances up.

Their boy stands
stock still in his faded, dirt-stained t-shirt,
watching me pass,

his eyes solemn with worry
like the eyes
of any young, wild thing.

At Harrison Flats,
the sky is cut by wires, and a combine
dies in a stubblefield.

I am numb.

I drive on
toward the house I live in
that is not mine,

and where,
so that I will never feel shame,
so that I will not dream,

you left
stalked and whiskered heads of wheat
in a rippled-glass pitcher

beside the door.

Passing through Albuquerque

At dusk, by the irrigation ditch
gurgling past backyards near the highway,
locusts raise a maze of calls in cottonwoods.

A Spanish girl in a white party dress
strolls the levee by the muddy water
where her small sister plunks in stones.

Beyond a low adobe wall and a wrecked car
men are pitching horseshoes in a dusty lot.
Someone shouts as he clangs in a ringer.

Big winds buffet in ahead of a storm,
rocking the immense trees and whipping up
clouds of dust, wild leaves, and cottonwool.

In the moment when the locusts pause and the girl
presses her up-fluttering dress to her bony knees
you can hear a banjo, guitar, and fiddle

playing "The Mississippi Sawyer" inside a shack.
Moments like that, you can love this country.

About the Editor . . .

Kurt Brown is founding director of the Aspen Writers' Conference, now in its eighteenth year, founding director of Writers' Conferences and Festivals (a national association of directors), now in its fourth year, past editor of *Aspen Anthology,* and past president of the Aspen Literary Foundation.

His poems have appeared in many literary periodicals, including the *Ontario Review,* the *Berkeley Poetry Review,* the *Seattle Review,* the *Southern Poetry Review,* the *Massachusetts Review,* the *Indiana Review,* and many others. He is the editor of two annuals, *The True Subject* (1993) and *Sex, Lies, and Poetry* (1994), which gather outstanding lectures from writers' conferences and festivals as part of the *Writers on Life & Craft Series,* published by Graywolf Press.

He is married and lives in Snowmass Village, Colorado, and Cambridge, Massachusetts.

ACKNOWLEDGMENTS

Agha Shahid Ali: "I See Chile in My Rearview Mirror" and "Snow on the Desert" from *A Nostalgist's Map of America* by Agha Shahid Ali. Copyright © 1991 by Agha Shahid Ali. Reprinted with the permission of W. W. Norton & Company, Inc.

A. R. Ammons: "Auto Mobile" from *The Selected Poems* by A. R. Ammons. Copyright © 1987 by A. R. Ammons. Reprinted with the permission of W. W. Norton & Company, Inc.

Shirley Bowers Anders: "The Bus Home" from *The Bus Home: Poems* by Shirley Bowers Anders. Copyright © 1986 by Shirley Bowers Anders. Reprinted with the permission of the University of Missouri Press.

Jon Anderson: "Rosebud" from *In Sepia* by Jon Anderson. Copyright © 1974 by Jon Anderson. Reprinted with the permission of The University of Pittsburgh Press.

Maggie Anderson: "Holding the Family Together" from *A Space Filled with Moving* by Maggie Anderson. Copyright © 1992 by Maggie Anderson. Reprinted with the permission of the University of Pittsburgh Press.

John Balaban: "Crossing West Nebraska, Looking for Blue Mountain," "Passing through Albuquerque," and "Riding Westward" from *Words for My Daughter* by John Balaban. Copyright © 1991 by John Balaban. Reprinted with the permission of Copper Canyon Press.

Lee Ballentine: "The Pileup" from *Dream Protocols* by Lee Ballentine. Copyright © 1992 by Lee Ballentine. Reprinted with the permission of Lee Ballentine and Talisman Press.

Stephen Berg: "Driving Out Again at Night" from *Grief* by Stephen Berg; published by Viking Penguin, a division of Penguin Books USA, Inc. Copyright © 1975 by Stephen Berg. Reprinted with the permission of Stephen Berg.

Bruce Berger: "Encounter," first appeared in *Four Quarters,* March 1969; "Great Basin Blues," was first published in *Counter/Measures,* 1974; "Phaëthon" (under the title "Driving into the Sun") and "Ranch Exit" appeared in *Aspen Anthology,* Spring 1977. All reprinted with the permission of Bruce Berger.

Elizabeth Bishop: "Filling Station" and "The Moose" from *The Complete Poems of Elizabeth Bishop* by Elizabeth Bishop. Copyright © 1933-1979 by Elizabeth Bishop; renewal copyright © 1980 by Alice Hellen Methfessel. Reprinted with the permission of Farrar, Straus & Giroux.

Robert Bly: "Driving toward the Lac Qui Parle River" from *Selected Poems* by Robert Bly. Copyright © 1986 by Robert Bly. Reprinted with the permission of Harper & Row.

Philip Booth: "Pickup" and "Zeros" from *Selves* by Philip Booth. Copyright ©

Index

Designed by Don Leeper.
Art by Kim David Cooper.
Typeset in Minion
by Stanton Publication Services.
Printed on acid-free Glatfelter Natural paper
by Princeton Academic Press.

More poetry anthologies from Milkweed Editions:

Clay and Star
Contemporary Bulgarian Poets
Translated and edited
by Lisa Sapinkopf and Georgi Belev

Looking for Home
Women Writing about Exile
Edited by Deborah Keenan and Roseann Lloyd

Minnesota Writes
Poetry
Edited by Jim Moore and Cary Waterman

Mixed Voices
Contemporary Poems about Music
Edited by Emilie Buchwald and Ruth Roston

Mouth to Mouth
Twelve Mexican Women Poets
Edited by Forrest Gander

Passages North Anthology
A Decade of Good Writing
Edited by Elinor Benedict

The Poet Dreaming in the Artist's House
Contemporary Poems about the Visual Arts
Edited by Emilie Buchwald and Ruth Roston

This Sporting Life
Contemporary American Poems
about Sports and Games
Edited by Emilie Buchwald and Ruth Roston